# WHIRLWINDS AND SMALL VOICES

# WHIRLWINDS AND SMALL VOICES

## Sustaining Commitment to Work with Special-Needs Children

Amy McConkey Robbins and Clarence McConkey

LUCAS PARK BOOKS

BOOKS

ST. LOUIS, MISSOURI

Original Celtic Mandala on cover by Elantu Veovode
Cover and Book Design by Dave Sindrey

All quotations from the Holy Bible come from the New Revised Standard Version (1989) unless otherwise noted.

ISBN: 978-1-60350-000-9-8

Published by Lucas Park Books
www.lucasparkbooks.com

*This book is dedicated to
the world-wide circle of those
who serve children with special needs
and
to the memory of
Joanne Myers McConkey
(1929 - 1973)*

# CONTENTS

# FOREWORD

*"Time lost is time when we have not lived a full
human life, time unenriched by experience,
creative endeavor, enjoyment, and suffering."*
-Dietrich Bonhoeffer

W ITH SPECIAL-NEEDS CHILDREN AS A FOCAL POINT, AMY MCCONKEY
Robbins and her father the Reverend Clarence McConkey combine the
perspectives of consummate professionals and caring human beings.
The special qualities that make us human include the development of language,
awareness of self, and the awareness of right and wrong.

The notion that God can work through adversity is a paradoxical concept.
According to C.S. Lewis in *The Problem Of Pain*, "If God were good, he would wish
to make his creatures perfectly happy…but the creatures are not happy." Resolution
of this dilemma requires a well-grounded spiritual perspective which the authors
willingly share.

Still small voices provide the serenity to deal with the confusing world of conflict-
ing priorities. Yet, another world of small voices is described in this book. These
are the small voices of the special-needs children who can change the world given
the ability to communicate. The development of communication skills is time sensitive and a window exists in early childhood which is forever lost if not nurtured.

The ability to synthesize time honored principles and new concepts requires risk
taking. Amy made a bold step early in her career, deviating from the tried-and-true
to explore the application of new technology and a novel approach to special-needs
children. In the process, she became the innovator of new assessment tools that are
now the standard in our field.

The concepts of creation and re-creation apply individually to the subject and
to the care giver but there is also a precious reciprocal relationship. This book is a
treasure that captures the essence of this relationship.

Richard T. Miyamoto, M.D., FACS, FAAP
Arilla Spence DeVault Professor & Chairman
Department of Otolaryngology-Head and Neck Surgery
Indiana University School of Medicine

# PREFACE

A S I WAS COLLECTING NOTES FOR THIS BOOK, LOOKING OVER MANY YEARS of entries in my daily journal, holding long conversations with my father and others in our profession, I have had a feeling of spiritual oneness with my colleagues. There are a lot of us in this business of helping children with special needs and their families. We're scattered all over the world. Yet I see us as a band of brothers and sisters engaged in a common task, helping children and their families toward a more satisfying life. I believe we are a part of a great circle of comradeship. I am proud to be part of such a universal community.

This book has been a labor of love. It's a product of things I've recorded in my journal going back a long while. In shaping these random thoughts and experiences I've had the presence of my father for guidance, for sharing his own life's spiritual journey and the flavoring of his humor, biblical knowledge and insight into human life. We laughed a lot as we worked together. Almost from the time I started studying Speech-Language Pathology, my father and I began long conversations about how the spiritual life of a clinician affects one's proficiency, objectivity and professionalism. As a pastoral counselor my father has had a special sensitivity to the role of spirituality in the life of clinicians. (While "clinician" is the word most associated with my particular work, we believe the themes we write about are relevant for people in many of the serving professions. Throughout the book, we have used a variety of terms to signify those in the "serving professions" in the hope that readers will feel an inclusive rather than exclusive approach to the themes we explore. ) Conversations my father and I have had over time have touched on themes such as faith and healing, therapy and holistic health as well as both positive and negative effects of spirituality in the lives of clinical workers. As a United Methodist minister, college teacher and author my father has been an invaluable guide in shaping my personal faith as it comes to bear on my clients. We, my father and I, have written this book together, and so both our names are listed as authors. Because his thinking and mine are so intertwined, the reader may notice a switching from the singular "I", when I write of my own clinical work, to the plural, "we" at other times. There was simply no way to separate the influence of my father on me (was this his idea or mine?), nor did I want to. As we worked on this project, I sensed my father's hand on my shoulder - sometimes physically, always metaphysically and spiritually.

You will soon find that my own journaling is a central aspect of this book. Actually, I also inherited journal keeping from my father. In my possession are many of the journals he kept over the years about his life, ministry and our family. They are precious documents of a life lived. Perhaps my own family will someday read my journals with the same sense of revelation. But my father and journaling have not been my only muses along the way. At every step I've tried to reflect the sense of wonder that I have found in great sources of renewal and inspiration from other writers, poets and theologians who wonder as they wander. The insights of these great thinkers have served as beacons, helping to guide me back again and again to the vocation to which I am called. I'll share these beacons with you as we walk through these seven days of Re-creation. My own journal entries, upon reflection, have served as beacons as well. These I will share as *italicized passages* marked by a creature that has always captured my attention, the hummingbird.

Together we've explored the deep connection between clinical work, the clinician and spiritual faith. As I look back over so many journal entries, I am astonished at how often my work and faith intersected. Faith is not some other-worldly package of perfection hanging around in the sky. Faith is what happens to us in our work, in our families and in our personal lives. When I write of my faith, I know through countless conversations that many others share similar thoughts and spiritual leanings without denominational or sectarian shadings. So just as each of us has a way of faith, this is a seven-day view of mine and in important aspects that of my father. We've tried to find a place in this book for this conviction as you and I live our lives day by day.

Thank you for coming with us.

# IN THE BEGINNING

# RE-CREATION AND STANDING IN THE "TRAGIC GAP"

TWO CENTRAL THEMES FLOW THROUGH THE PAGES OF THIS BOOK: THE RE-Creation of the clinician, and standing in "the tragic gap" as described by Parker Palmer. For the first theme, Re-creation, I use the seven days of Creation as a metaphor for the cycle of life, the seven days of the week that each of us experiences as a clinician and a person. The seven days of Creation have always been for me a symbol for the origins of everything because it was done as the poets and priests understood, in an orderly cycle. There was the first day, then the second and third day in order, a cycle, a rhythm. Everything I know about today is subject to this cycling of birth and death, creating and recreating, pulsing to the throb of the Original Pulse. Time has a rhythm: centuries, years, months, seconds. There is a cycle of seasons; winter, spring, summer, fall. As the writer of Ecclesiastes knew, "For everything there is a season, and a time for every purpose under heaven."

Our journey has been lived day by day. Each day has been a rising up in the morning and lying down at night, of eating rituals, work schedules, family times, worship practices and all the rest that make up daily life. The more I've contemplated our dependence on the predictable, the more I'm drawn to the inexhaustible riches of the first two chapters of Genesis. At the risk of anthropomorphism, I've sometimes wondered if, in creating things, God might have kept a journal. Perhaps with the enormity of what had to be done he might have forgotten if he had planned to make those iguanas on Tuesday or Friday. Nothing wrong with a heavenly Journal! In fact, that's exactly what we have in those two chapters that begin the Bible. The Creation Story found there is sacred to Christians, Jews and Muslims and even to those without a demonstrable religious faith, at least a source of adventure. If God doesn't mind that I've established here a parallel in my journal keeping with his, (yes, I am using the male gender for God but I am perfectly at home with the concept of God as female) then what I write on every page is only commentary on what he and the ancient Hebrew priests and prophets knew long ago. "I Wonder as I Wander out under the sky" we sing at Christmas. We've been given the capacity to wonder, to think, to appreciate, to be guided and enriched by all created things. In this spirit of wonder and awe I live in this world, as a wanderer, a pilgrim, a novice, wondering all the while at its simple immensity. "Out under the sky" is emblematic of my journey.

"Sometimes I'm up, sometimes I'm down," is our story, yours and mine. As I read and re-read the Creation story I have realized that this wonderful drama parallels my spiritual re-creation story. I look at my life, the journey I've taken in my profession, my family life and my community involvements. From my journal, my memories and knowledge of the pitfalls and challenges of this profession of helping special-needs children, I see an intersection of the 7-day cycle of the Genesis Creation story and my own 7-day cycle as a clinician and a person of faith. Therefore, each of these days and their themes comprise the chapters of this book:

## The First Day
*Creation of Light; Re-creation of Vocation*

## The Second Day
*Creation of Water; Re-creation after Discouragement*

## The Third Day
*Creation of Plant Life; Re-creation of Personal Relationships and Family Life*

## The Fourth Day
*Creation of the Seasons: Re-creation within Conflict*

## The Fifth day
*Creation of the Animal Kingdom: Re-creation of Inspiration*

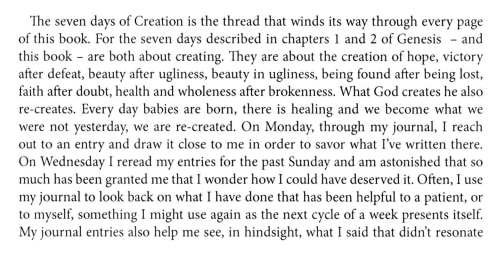

## The Sixth Day
*Creation of Man and Woman: Re-creation of Gratitude*

## The Seventh Day
*Creation of Sabbath; Re-creation of Faith\**

The seven days of Creation is the thread that winds its way through every page of this book. For the seven days described in chapters 1 and 2 of Genesis – and this book – are both about creating. They are about the creation of hope, victory after defeat, beauty after ugliness, beauty in ugliness, being found after being lost, faith after doubt, health and wholeness after brokenness. What God creates he also re-creates. Every day babies are born, there is healing and we become what we were not yesterday, we are re-created. On Monday, through my journal, I reach out to an entry and draw it close to me in order to savor what I've written there. On Wednesday I reread my entries for the past Sunday and am astonished that so much has been granted me that I wonder how I could have deserved it. Often, I use my journal to look back on what I have done that has been helpful to a patient, or to myself, something I might use again as the next cycle of a week presents itself. My journal entries also help me see, in hindsight, what I said that didn't resonate

**\* Readers will note that the day of the week corresponding to the "Sabbath" differs between Christians and Jews, and even between some Christian denominations. There's no way I can or want to dilute the distinctiveness and richness of the Sabbath in any of these religious traditions. However, I have conceived this book from my own practice. Thus, Sunday completes the cycle of my work week and is my Sabbath before the week begins again on Monday, which I designate as the First Day, and so on.**

with a colleague or what I tried that didn't work with a patient, and how I might improve the next week, the next appointment. As S. Blanton, M.D. has written, "To be happy, drop the words, 'if only' and substitute instead the words, 'next time.'" I am thankful that the cycle of Re-Creation God provides gives us the opportunity for this next time. As a therapist, a person, a wife and mother, a friend, a church member, I know how my life is inextricably bound to the seven days of Creation. I practice a cycle of rituals for Monday, Tuesday, Saturday, for Sunday. I cannot escape this circling of days nor do I want to; there is something dependable, even prophetic, in knowing Sunday is going to come on Sunday and not on Tuesday. But the story of creation under no circumstances ends at the conclusion of Chapter 1 of Genesis. Everything that comes after is another story of Re-creation, Deliverance, Redemption, Forgiveness, Reconciliation and Renewal, and above all, Hope.

We who share this common cause of caring for children and their families are also works in progress. This brings me to a second theme of this book, the notion described by Parker Palmer of "standing in the tragic gap" between the hard reality in which we live on the one hand, and what we know to be possible on the other. On several days in the seven-day cycle of Re-creation, I want to discuss how prevalent this gap is for clinicians, yet offer the confidence that we have the courage and capacity to stand in this gap and thus, to become agents of new ideas and possibilities.

In writing about my personal spiritual journey I have remembered how that path has involved many types of whirlwinds: the weary dizziness of being overextended, the unsure footing of earthquakes from having done something poorly, and the disorienting smoke from fires that can happen at work, within the family and in community commitments. Caught up in these confusing whirlwinds and fires I have wasted time, done less than I could have, suffered anxiety and regret, and have often come away with feelings of dissatisfaction. The saving grace given to me in the midst of these storms has been those moments when I have taken time to listen to the still small voices available to me. These voices were my conscience, my soul, dedication to my vocation, advice from those wiser than I am, prayer for guidance and serenity, trust in my religious faith to set me aright and the good sense to listen. My personal faith is always a contest between whirlwinds and small voices.

I am not alone in these tensions. Isn't that the nature of being human, of our vocation? I know, too, that I draw inspiration from that magnetic man, Elijah, as we find him in 1 Kings 19. Elijah, a prophet struggling to be faithful to God in a time of change and challenge, comes before God to complain of these perplexities in his personal life. He expresses himself as being both inadequate and unworthy. God answers that Elijah should separate himself for a time from these confusions in a secret place apart, in this case a cave. While Elijah waits there for further guidance, a whirlwind sweeps by and the prophet assumes the mighty wind is God showing himself. But God is not in the whirlwind. An earthquake shakes the earth but God is not in the earthquake. After this, a fire consumes the landscape but God is not in the fire. Then, a still small voice is heard and in that voice God reveals himself to the prophet.

In one sense, this is a story about whirlwinds, earthquakes and fires that we all deal with in our lives. It is also about the still small voice. In my own life this still small voice of guidance, comfort, insight and renewal has come through prayer and meditation, in quiet times, in solitude and in Bible reading, and in worship in our family church. In a way this is a sojourn into my own spiritual cave. This is mostly what we write about in this book and it is why we give the book its title.

In these writings, we use the term spirituality as it describes our connection to what is Infinite, Transcendent, to what is beyond earth and this earthly life, to what is higher, deeper and richer than creeds, liturgies and buildings. These are components of spirituality for many of us but not spirituality itself. Spirituality is a Presence within us, Immanence, an indwelling Spirit, Mystery, Awe, Enlightenment, Solemnity. Spirituality is Wisdom as the Gnostics understood it, God as Jesus understood it, the "High and Lifted Up" as Isaiah understood it; Allah as Muhammad understood it, the Holy Spirit as countless Christians understand it. When I personally express in and through my life the essentials of this spirituality I express it as the daily loving of God, as Christ centered in word and deed and sustained by the unfaltering Christian hope that is both temporal and eternal. I have never felt that spirituality was the same as "churchiosity." I hasten to add however that the church to which my family and I belong (United Methodist) is one of my greatest stimulations to deeper faith and belief. Our church, whose motto is, "…where spiritual journeys meet" is an open, inclusive, musically dynamic fellowship, interracial, filled with a lively and energetic spirit life. While this church is not the source of my faith, it enhances it richly.

The American poet, Emily Dickinson, uses a phrase in one of her poems that seems to capture the nature of my own spiritual life. Dickinson refers to "….a certain slant of light, on Winter afternoons….." These slants of light are at the heart of any person's spiritual life. By this I mean that none of us lives up there in the clouds of some perfect harmony with God, as if we were saints constantly filled with nothing but inspiration from on high. Witness the lives of the great saints of the church. Oh, my, how they struggled! I've always thought of the spiritual life as a life of slants, a moment of insight here, a feeling of the nearness of God there, a worship service that means something special, the lifting up of our faith through music, great feelings of beauty that come from poetry, prayer, something we read, something we hear, little moments where we know for sure God is touching us with his love and forgiveness and renewing energy. Scott Russell Sanders in his *Private History of Awe* writes of these slants of light in slightly different language, explaining that though the divine is grounded and sustains everything, it reveals itself, "only in flashes, like a darkened landscape lit by lightning." We live in the real world after all and sometimes our work, family life, moments of discouragement, times of loneliness, disappointment, hurt feelings, make for less than spiritual ecstasy. Like Scott, I depend on these slants of light for inward peace and consolation. Emily Dickinson helps me with this too. There are others, a call from a colleague will do it, a word of appreciation from a parent, the voice of happiness from a child, a good progress report from that child's teacher, a shaft of pleasure from my family, moments of inner peace for tasks well done, these are some of the others. There are many of them.

Not in a thousand years is my journey yours. We each travel our own way, down our own path to faith and belief, the way of the Pilgrim. Pema Chodron, an American Buddhist nun reminds us that the most important element of being on a spiritual path is "just to keep moving!" My grandmother Ocie McConkey, who came to the Kansas prairie from Virginia in about 1901 and lived to be 97 years old, would express the same thing in slightly different words. When asked how she was doing, her answer was usually, "Oh, jist trying to keep a-goin." I share with you by way of this book those insights that have kept me moving, kept me a-goin,' that have lighted my path and my journey, insights that are precious to me. I offer this in the same spirit you would offer your insights to me.

# THE FIRST DAY

## RE-CREATION OF VOCATIONAL COMMITMENT

*"Then God said, 'Let there be light,' and there was light. Then he separated the light from the darkness." Gen.1:3*

*"The lines have fallen for me in pleasant places..." Ps.16:6*

*New Every Morning*

*Every day is a fresh beginning,*
*Listen, my soul, to the glad refrain.*
*And in spite of old sorrows*
*And older sinning*
*Troubles forecasted*
*And possible pain,*
*Take heart with the day and begin again.*
        *-Susan Coolidge*

*I wake up each day wanting, hoping, praying to relate more ad-*
*equately to my patients, colleagues, mentors and to God. Each of*
*these relationships is important to me; each is a part of the bond*
*with which we are entrusted when we enter our profession. My*
*sense of the sacred nature of these relationships is enriched by the*
*learned and wise counsel of Rabbi Elazar ben Sammua who has*
*written, "Let the honor of your student be as dear to you as your*
*own, and the honor of your colleague be like the reverence due to*
*your teacher, and the reverence for your teacher be like the rever-*
*ence for Heaven." [Ethics of the Fathers, Phillip Birnbaum (Ed.),*
*NY: Hebrew Publishing Co, 1949, p. 32.]*

# *Cycles and Circles*

GOD MUST HAVE HAD CONFIDENCE IN CYCLES AND CIRCLES. HE CERTAIN-LY made good use of them when He created things in the Beginning: "It is He who sits above the circle of the earth..." (Is. 40:22). Anne Morrow Lindbergh in her slim treasure of a book, *Gift from the Sea*, refers to the pattern of our life as circular and evokes the image of spokes on a wheel. As with so many other writers, modern and ancient, she speaks of the repetition, the re-cycling of thoughts, emotions and energy that exist in life. This same emphasis on circles is found in the haunting words of the great Sioux nation leader, Black Elk, when re-cordings were made of him in 1930 by the poet laureate of the state of Nebraska, John Neihardt. Black Elk, old and nearly blind, was interviewed on the Rosebud Reservation. When I read these interviews in *Black Elk Speaks*, I had the conviction that somehow, even all these years later, I was in the presence of a great spiritual master. "You have noticed," Black Elk said, "that everything an Indian does is in a circle and that is because the Power of the World always works in circles, and ev-erything tries to be round. Even the seasons form a great circle in their changing, and always come back to.....the sacred, unbroken round hoop." As one who works with children, this is the renewal, the regeneration that is the circle of time in a day,

15

when I can try to have more patience in the afternoon than I had in the morning; the circle of a week that gives me another chance to do a better job with a patient during the appointment next week, the circle of a season, of a year, and so on. I have a place of mini-retreat where I begin each day – to think, pray, to write in my journal.

*In this place early this morning, the daily cycle of my keeping covenant with God, imperfect as it is, begins as I rise from the night. I have a busy day of work ahead of me. This first day of the week, the first day of Creation, begins like most days - on my knees for a moment of prayer and contemplation. This is a good habit, I learned it from my childhood. I kneel to receive communion in our church, I knelt for the blessing for my marriage, I have knelt in churches where my family and I have visited. If I kneel just at the right moment of the early sunrise and the right time of the season I can see a stream of light, the exact dimensions of the window panes, come into my room at an angle to anchor itself on the floor beside me. In this ray of light a myriad of dust particles float softly and gently in the motionless air. I watch them as they glide in the silence, descending, moving from the upper light to the darkened floor below. I think, how like God's renewing gifts, these minute particles of assurance, small blessings, easily grasped messages of forgiveness, understanding and acceptance. This is my chance, perhaps my only chance in this busy day, to center myself. Cycles and circles, the repetition of time and weeks and seasons, is important to me. If I miss the opportunity to make the most of one Monday God will (hopefully) forgive my neglect and give me another Monday to make amends. If I fail to appreciate the laughter of one of my small patients who doesn't have much to laugh about I pray I will be given another chance to listen for it, and respond to it in the next appointment.*

*If I ever thought life on this earth didn't offer unlimited possibilities of renewal and regeneration, if I ever thought this whole business of things being made over again wasn't real, I would be so despondent. I don't know how I could remain committed to the difficult work that is my vocation, or continue to have patience with special-needs children and their parents. But I look upon this renewal as a vital part of the process of Creation and re-Creation. The Book of Lamentations reminds us, "The promises of God are renewed every morning," (3:23), and one of the things I always have in mind when I come to these early morning meditations is to ask for those promises to be renewed in my life.*

# First Brushes with Vocation

O N THIS FIRST DAY OF THE CYCLE OF CREATION, OF CREATING, I REALIZE HOW strongly I depend on this re-creation for my commitment to children with special needs. And I think back to the first encounters I had with what was to become my life's vocation. This happened when I was just 6 or 7 years old. Growing up in the 1960s, there was no mandated public education for special-needs children and therefore, many of my friends had never met such children. While I was still in elementary school I used to help out in the summer at a day care program in my father's church, St. James United Methodist Church in Bellevue, Nebraska. This program, funded by the March of Dimes, was the only church-sponsored program, and one of the few programs that even existed in our community, for special-needs children in the early 1960's. I can still picture in my mind the little boy with developmental delays whom, I guess, could be considered my first student. He was very small for his age, wore heavy brown orthopedic shoes and stayed glued to my side whenever I was there. He was compliant and cheerful as long as he could twirl a dandelion in his hand. We would play together and sing songs or do art projects during the sessions, then I would pick up that little dandelion-twirling boy and carry him to the car and his waiting mother. He would twirl that dandelion a mile a minute and I knew it was a symbol of his joyous anticipation of reunion.

Today, as I sometimes do on Monday mornings, I feel an energy, a spirit of excitement that I have the week ahead to see my patients, to observe progress in them, to watch a language milestone finally achieved, to learn a student struggling academically has managed to pass the state academic proficiency exam, to see a mother laugh again months after hearing the diagnosis of autism spectrum disorder. My vocation beckons on these days. Random House unabridged dictionary defines "vocation" as, "a strong impulse or inclination to follow a particular career; a call or summons [strong language that]; a function to which one is called by God." On a good Monday, I feel something akin to what I felt when I became acquainted with special-needs children, first as a child in the church program I've mentioned, and then at Hollins College. I don't think my interest fell into the category of "divine summons" at either of those points, but rather, "the strong impulse or inclination to follow a particular career." (I want to write more about that later – the maturity of our sense of vocation.) Sometimes, the concept of vocation is perfectly expressed for me in the words of Robert Louis Stevenson: "To know what you prefer instead of humbly saying Amen to what the world tells you you should prefer, is to keep your soul alive."

# Vocation Takes Root at a Stuttering Clinic

MY FIRST FEW DAYS AT HOLLINS WERE SPENT IN FRESHMAN ORIENTATION where new students became acquainted with work going on at the college. The campus was buzzing with excitement at that time, anticipating the publication of recent Hollins graduate Annie Dillard's first book, *Pilgrim at Tinker Creek*, for which she would be awarded the Pulitzer Prize during our Sophomore year. Annie was married to a Hollins English professor and so was on campus all the time. In any case, as part of the freshman orientation, I attended a lecture by Dr. Ronald Webster who had developed a new and nationally-recognized technique, the Fluency Shaping Program (FSP) to treat severe adult stutterers successfully. His lab and clinic were located on the Hollins campus in Roanoke, Virginia. After his lecture, I asked him if I could volunteer at his clinic and he agreed. Within a week, I knew this was something I could probably do with my life – mind you, there have been many variations along the way: I left the field of stuttering, I haven't worked with adults in 20 years, I no longer work in a clinic but in private practice - yet the spark was ignited there as I watched adult stutterers whose disability was so severe they could not speak at all under normal circumstances.

Part of my job at the stuttering clinic was to make a two-minute pre-treatment video recording in which patients were to say, "My name is ____ _____" and then to describe a bit about themselves. I had instructions to run the tape for two minutes for each patient, and many of them never made it through the first sentence because of their dysfluencies. I held the camera as they agonized over and over to get out those five words, "My name is ____ _____", and I wasn't allowed to help them because this was our baseline against which to measure later progress. I saw these adults trapped inside themselves. After the patients spent an intensive 12-hour per day, three-week therapy course, I made the post-treatment video, before the patients left to go back to their homes. One of the young men who had never completed even his first sentence on the pre-treatment tape was Daniel, a 20-year old student from Princeton. Three weeks later, on his post-treatment tape, he talked on and on (using the newly-acquired slow and gentle-onset speech techniques, mind you), about his life and experience with the Fluency Program. "How do you think things might be different now that you can speak fluently?" I asked. I'll never forget his answer. "It's just that now, I'll be able to ask questions," he replied. A brilliant and witty young man, he had attended classes at Princeton for two years without ever making a single comment or asking a question. He and I both knew he could now give voice to the thoughts that previously had been trapped inside him. This change would finally allow others to see and hear him as he really was – all of him – even his masterful verbal wit. If I had any doubt about my vocation (at least as an inclination then, not a summons) it was decided that day. I wonder how I would have reacted then to read in Isaiah 50:4 when the Servant declares, "The Lord has given me the tongue of a teacher……" (NIV).

# Hearing and Voices

CLEARLY MY VOCATION AS A SPEECH-LANGUAGE PATHOLOGIST WORKING PRImarily with hearing-impaired children is concerned with the development and restoration of hearing and of the voice. Equally clear is that this vocation is intimately connected to the "still, small voice" I hear inside me and try to obey. The enormity of what it means to teach someone to communicate is as powerful an inspiration to me now, almost 30 years later, as it was back at Hollins College. Helene Cixous wrote, "To think we have at our disposal the biggest thing in the Universe, and that is language. What one can do with language is…..infinite."

Many colleagues have shared stories with me of how they came to the field of teaching, or audiology, or otolaryngology. Some say they stumbled into our vocation, but others have told me they recognized - they had an ah-ha moment - This is what I want to do with my life's work. My colleague, Maura Berntsen and I have had many discussions about our work, the larger meaning in what we do, and she has given me permission to share the experience, in her own words, of her vocational calling.

Maura writes:

> As a 15 year-old, I had never heard of deaf education and thought that I would someday be a doctor or a journalist. A group from my high school visited several universities in St. Louis, including Fontbonne College. I had this notion of going to a larger university in St. Louis because my grandfather had attended Medical School there – but when I visited Fontbonne, it felt like home. My group's guide, Marybeth was majoring in Deaf Education and excitedly talked about what her studies were preparing her to do, and I was fascinated. My mom says that she still remembers me coming home and talking about it and that she knew then I would end up studying deaf education. I guess I was in the right place at the right time to hear my call to this field. Now, all these years and hundreds of deaf children later, there are days when I get discouraged or frustrated because I'm not able to connect with a child and family or the staff I work with seems unhappy with their situations. But then I take a deep breath, usually talk to God, and then someone will say something that helps me remember why I am here. I can't really think of a time when I have thought that I made the wrong choice. I have been graced with the opportunity to be with families when they understand sound and language for the first time. I am able to meet with decision makers who can better the lives of children and families. I find that a "chance" meeting between a college senior and high school sophomore

has led me to experience so many tiny miracles. I may not always see things this way at difficult moments in my work, but when I witness families and children building relationships and shared communication, despite the presence of a significant hearing loss, I know that I am exactly where I am supposed to be.

## Ups and Downs of Vocational Commitment

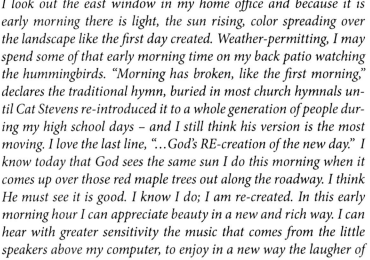

*I look out the east window in my home office and because it is early morning there is light, the sun rising, color spreading over the landscape like the first day created. Weather-permitting, I may spend some of that early morning time on my back patio watching the hummingbirds. "Morning has broken, like the first morning," declares the traditional hymn, buried in most church hymnals until Cat Stevens re-introduced it to a whole generation of people during my high school days – and I still think his version is the most moving. I love the last line, "…God's RE-creation of the new day." I know today that God sees the same sun I do this morning when it comes up over those red maple trees out along the roadway. I think He must see it is good. I know I do; I am re-created. In this early morning hour I can appreciate beauty in a new and rich way. I can hear with greater sensitivity the music that comes from the little speakers above my computer, to enjoy in a new way the laugher of the children who wait at the bus stop across the road.*

I FEEL THE POWER OF THIS RE-CREATION AND FIND ENERGY IN THE POEM BY Susan Coolidge, "New Every Morning," that opened this chapter. It is especially moving to start my day saying this poem, knowing it is used in hospice care in the United Kingdom. "Every day is a fresh beginning, Listen, my soul, to the glad refrain….Take heart with the day and begin again." On good Mondays, I can recapture, almost re-create that feeling at first realizing what I was meant to do, or what Maura has described above. Just as God created Light and it illuminated the first day of Creation, so I can sometimes re-create these enlightenments leading to my vocation. I can relate to the instruction of Gautama Buddha that, "Your work is to discover your work and then with all your heart to give yourself to it." Enlightenments are easy on the days they fall into your lap. Like the recent school journal entry shared by one of my 10-year old students, Colleen*. Born deaf but thriving now in regular school with two cochlear implants, she and her class were asked to write what one physical aspect of themselves they would change. Colleen wrote, "If I could change one physical aspect of myself it would be my nose. I want to change my nose so I wouldn't have to smell a bad smell again. Everything I sniff would be my favorite smell. My favorite smell is actually the smell of roses, it just smells so good!" No mention of deafness, ears, or the hearing devices she wears.

**\* All patients' names have been changed throughout the book**

Just her nose. How can I not love going to work on days when I teach children such as Colleen?

But sometimes I struggle to create vocational enthusiasm, or simply cannot do it. I'll write later about the challenges, discouragements and just plain hassles that wear us down, eat away at us, take the pleasure from our work. I spoke in the previous chapter about Parker Palmer's concept of standing in the "the tragic gap," the gap that will never disappear between the hard realities of life and work, and the way we know things could be. [To hear a podcast of Palmer's discussion of this topic, go to: www.couragerenewal.org/podcast/tragic_gap.] Palmer explains that the gap "….. isn't tragic because it is sad but because it is inevitable. It will never be otherwise." He challenges us to examine how we can faithfully hold the tension between reality, flawed as it is, and the possibilities that exist in an ideal world. This is not a rhetorical discussion. One of the most important, pragmatic qualities a person can have is the capacity to stand in the tragic gap. Standing there means you hold in delicate balance the opposing forces of radical opposites. If you lean too far to the "tragic" side, you can become disillusioned or cynical, become the victim, adopt the attitude, "I can make no difference. The problems are too tough to tackle. I'll just put my time in at this clinic until I retire." If, on the other hand, you try to fill the huge gap by leaning too far to the "what could be" side, you become an irrelevant idealist who is so far removed from reality that you can't relate to the world as it actually is. The result of leaning too far either way, says Palmer, is that you become ineffective and/or disengaged. But those who are able to stand courageously in the tension of the tragic gap may become agents for positive change and renewal.

This notion of the tragic gap resonates when I discern in myself cynical feelings, though usually this is temporary. The danger is that cynicism for any of us may creep in slowly, then with more vigor, and for some may lead to disillusion with the profession or a decision to leave the field entirely. I have seen first hand several gifted clinicians who just couldn't reconcile the vocational call with the real world they had to navigate when working with children with special needs. A sobering fact is that 50% of first-year teachers are no longer in the profession after five years. I must say that this is a significant part of my and my father's decision to write this book – we believe that re-creation of vocational summons is possible! There is re-creating: a new vocational commitment can arise from a person who has grown weary and cynical. The beginning of this day, this first day of creation, also holds the possibility of re-creation, renewal, restoration.

## A Pearl Behind the Anguish

I MENTIONED ANNE MORROW LINDBERGH EARLIER, AND HOW HER BOOK HAS inspired millions of people with its simple explanation of how shells from the sea can reveal profound secrets about life and how God moves in our lives with His power of re-creation. In some of those shells resides the reclusive oyster. There is a poignant account of oysters and the pain an oyster goes through in producing a pearl. You and I may wear a string of pearls, or earrings, without ever remembering those pearls were produced by suffering. More and more I've thought about the children that I've known over the years of my practice who live in pain of various kinds. We all know our patients who live with cognitive, emotional or physical disabilities. We dare not deny that they and their families suffer.

Yet I remember how many of those children come to me with a happy face and with pleasure even in their small achievements and I think at what cost of pain they show that happy face. In a lecture I attended a couple of years ago given by famed educator, Jonathan Kozol, I was moved as he spoke of teaching first graders in an inner-city school, and the tremendous weight of responsibility he felt when his little students looked up to him and trusted him and expected him to do the right thing, to make the right decisions about everything. Howard Arnold Walter, an American theologian and poet begins, "My Creed", with the line, "I would be true, for there are those who trust me." I feel ashamed sometimes that I so take for granted the trust my little patients place in me. Their small voices resonate in my head in the evening, as I think back on my day's work. And sometimes their words haunt me, like the six-year old boy who told me, his voice quivering, "My teacher yelled at me because she forgot to know that I can't read." Anguish is what I felt. I think of how my patients strive to please me in their progress with communication, how they may arrive for their session and eagerly say, "Listen, Miss Amy," then proudly pronounce a word we've been struggling with in speech therapy, a word they have finally managed to say correctly since our last session. Word by word, voice by voice, sentence by sentence, they are becoming, quite literally, new creations as a result of their linguistic abilities. These are "pearls of great price" that come from their pain. But through the pain, pearls of joy come to my patients and to me.

*Here at this morning hour I think of John O'Donohue's book, Beauty: The Invisible Embrace, how O'Donohue writes that we were created to be creators and at its very core, the purpose of creation is to serve and to evoke beauty. Am I not called to do this with the children and families who come to me in trust? As I let the spirit of this Creation day lift me up from the lethargy of the night I just have to ask the Lord to make me more sensitive to the pearl that lies behind the anguish of some of my little charges. I think Anne Morrow Lindbergh would like me doing that. Thank you, Lord, for giving me enough sense to see the pearls that are forming. Thank you, Anne.*

# Niko

This morning I will see Niko and his mother. Niko is a wonderfully bright child, responsive and eager. They always ask for early morning appointments and for that I am grateful because I love to start my day with Niko's infectious personality. He wore glasses until undergoing two eye surgeries, has a cochlear implant in each ear but none of this seems to bother him or slow him down. On the contrary the fitting of the cochlear implants has opened up the world of sound to him and his speech skills have exploded. What he used to communicate by pointing, a single sign or even a tantrum is now expressed in full sentences, almost all of which are understandable. Now four years old, he spends half his day in a special class and half-day in a community preschool. We expect that by Kindergarten, he will be ready to integrate fully into his neighborhood school.

I started seeing Niko after he came to his parents in Indianapolis at 11 months of age from an overseas orphanage. His deafness had not been diagnosed until after he arrived, and his parents were told that his "lazy eye" would need to be corrected with surgery. I watch with wonder and respect the way Niko's mother works with him, encourages him and follows through at home with the suggestions and activities provided them.

What a privilege it is to travel alongside families in their journey to a creative day for their children. Niko's parents and others have allowed me to share with them intimate moments of joy and sorrow, fear and celebration. In my early days as a clinician I avoided conversations with parents that might touch on these emotions, mostly because I was uncomfortable with my own feelings and how to react to theirs. Now I consider my relationship with parents to be a sacred gift. When families such as Niko's are receptive, I gently probe the emotional and spiritual sides of their journey with their child. Niko's mother has shared her insights with me. Recently she shared , "I think at first we went through the 'why' stage with God. I finally realized, though, that this was Niko's life journey and that God did make him a perfect little guy, we just had to do a few 'work-arounds' to help him hear with a cochlear implant. I can't imagine him being a more perfect child - being deaf is who he is. He is already an inspiration to a lot of people whom he meets, even at his young age of four." How I am humbled by the wisdom of this mother and so many others with whom I work. This morning, as many mornings, I pray the prayer of Marian Wright Edelman, "Lord, bless me with usefulness today."

# Mourning Doves

*When the first light of day creeps on the horizon, I'm sometimes transported back to my Grandma Ocie's house in western Kansas. In the summer time sleeping in the attic with four cousins per bed I would sometimes awaken to the sound of the mourning doves.*

*Their cooing, haunting but exquisite, was a sound implanted on my memory as strongly as if I were hearing them this very instant. If I think back to those Kansas summer mornings in bed with my cousins, the memory of the mourning dove resonates in my head and I hear the words of the song, "On the wings of a snow white dove, He sent his pure sweet Love, A sign from above, On the wings of a dove." The call of the mourning dove ushered in the light of a new day.*

## *Darkness and Light*

Y ET, IN THE MIDST OF ALL THAT LIGHT ON THE FIRST DAY OF CREATION there was also darkness. And there is darkness on days when I struggle to find meaning in what I do; sometimes I think I don't have the energy to work with another difficult child, I wonder if I should just cancel all my patients for the next day; I'm tempted to ignore the phone call from the clearly-irritated school administrator or the insurance company because I know full well the red-tape and run-around I'm going to encounter, feeling more and more frustrated at the waste of time and energy. And yet I go on, just as the poem says, "….in spite of old sorrows and older sinning, troubles forecasted and possible pain…" I know deep down that this is what I am meant to do, called to do. But it's more than that. Because, ironically, it is at these moments when I feel least committed, when I'm barely holding it together, that I am are actually on the brink of a potentially life-altering precipice, an abyss. At those moments, I have the most opportunity of finding healing and the fortitude to press onward in my work. In a recent retreat in which I was privileged to take part, Rick Jackson, co-director of the Center for Courage and Renewal said something that has stuck with me. Rick said, "The reasons people leave [the helping professions] are right next to the reasons they stay in them." This speaks to me of the energy that is created in both uplifting and frustrating situations. How can we harness this energy for the spreading of light rather than darkness? Pema Chodron writes that, "The only time we ever know what's really going on is when the rug's been pulled out and we can't find anywhere to land. We use these situations either to wake ourselves up or to put ourselves to sleep. Right now, in the very instant of groundlessness, is the seed of taking care of those who need our care and of discovering our goodness" (p. 9).

And in times of darkness when I question whether I want to go on with this vocation, I rely upon a storehouse of images, letters and stories that I keep as a way to re-new my inspiration. My mother told us a story once that I have never forgotten, I think she had read in a national magazine of some kind. It was about a railroad engineer guiding his train through the night in the face of a torrential thunderstorm. Battered by rain and wind, the engineer kept his eyes on the rails ahead of him as best he could, the only light in the darkness being the beam from the front of the cab. As the train pushed through the night the engineer suddenly saw ahead of him, stretching out across the wall of water and fog, a pair of gigantic wings, like angel's wings he said later. The wings hovered ahead of the train moving forward with the momentum of the train. The engineer, receptive to mystery and intuition, stopped the train to investigate the nature of the wings. He found that a moth had been impaled on the veering glass of the headlight beam, the light projecting the shadow of the small moth out onto the wall of fog and weather, many times magnified. Finding the source of the covering wings he also found he had stopped his train on the rim of an abyss.

> *Darkness sometimes lights us away from danger, to safety. Here in this little grotto-to-be I think of my imperfections, my less than right attitudes, my need for greater spiritual sensitivity, and a deeper sense of appreciation for just the simple act of touching the switch that brings all the light of the world into this room. I kneel, I ask the Giver of Light and Darkness to excise all joylessness from the beauty of this morning sky and from my life. As Og Mandino wrote, "I will love the light for it shows me the way. Yet, I will endure the darkness for it shows me the stars."*

## Sources of Vocational Renewal

WHERE DOES THE CLINICIAN LOOK FOR VOCATIONAL RENEWAL WHEN IT seems lost or weakening? Of course we all have our ways of creating renewal. For some it is through music, for some reading, others find it outdoors or writing or movies or white water rafting. At the end of this chapter, and every chapter, we offer suggestions clinicians may find helpful for renewing vocational commitment. We have provided ideas for those who read this book alone, and a second set of ideas for those who read this in a group setting. For me, renewal is so often found in two places: poetry and relationship. As for the first, it seems that, in a few, carefully-chosen words, the poet can capture what I either ruminate about in my mind with no resolution, or blather about verbally but am unable to express. The works of the Chilean poet, Pablo Neruda, have spoken to me since I first read his poetry at Balboa High School in the Panama Canal Zone where my family lived during my teenage years. My recommitment to my chosen vocation, my awareness of the light that, though temporarily covered, can be re-discovered, is expressed brilliantly in Neruda's short poem:

> *If each day falls*
> *inside each night,*
> *there exists a well*

*where clarity is imprisoned.*
*We need to sit on the rim*
*of the well of darkness*
*and fish for fallen light*
*with patience.*
  *- Neruda*

The light is there all along, Neruda seems to be saying. It has not disintegrated, but has fallen in a well of darkness, just as the original inspiration for my work, vocational commitment - may have fallen into a well of complacency, boredom, or more often, a frenetic, overwhelming schedule that masks the real reason I came into this profession in the first place. I must patiently, he emphasizes (gosh, does Neruda know who he's talking to when he says "with patience?") sit at the well of darkness, and search again for that fallen light, that lost inspiration because it's there, maybe deep in the well, but still there. An essential part of practicing that patience for me is prayer. For others, it may be meditation. But in any case, this patience is the conscious letting go of the need for control, a surrender to the willingness to be patient enough to find that fallen light again, knowing it is there, somewhere.

## Relationships

OVER THE YEARS, MY WORK HAS BECOME MORE ABOUT RELATIONSHIPS THAN about technique. At least, I've learned that the techniques, even the most advanced technologies, are only as good as the relationship we can create with the families of our special-needs children. But some would say it is much more than that – it is actually a necessary part of the health care worker's ability to successfully treat a child and his family.  Paul Brenner, M.D., and author of *Buddha in the Waiting Room* has observed over the years that when he is on vacation, some of his patients will be treated by his medical partners but will return later, saying they are not feeling better. Brenner will follow up by prescribing the identical treatment and the patients get better. Brenner asserts that healing, at least for some people, is dependent upon a trusting relationship between the healer and the patient. Brenner writes, "Trust has a healing effect because it creates an emotional response."

Should we wonder at this? Haven't we learned the nature of trust between a child and the child's parent? Isn't trust the cement that holds marriage together, gives people confidence in their elected leaders, makes possible the nearly unbreakable bond between a pastor and people of a church. Trust breeds confidence and confidence is one of the strongest impulses for hope, healing, courage and perseverance. The believer trusts the divine source of his faith and that trust is a power that can overcome even the world.

The intimacy with which some families allow us to touch their lives is a privilege. That is my vocation now: reaching children because I have reached their parents. In these tender, intimate moments, I know a little of what my father has experienced his whole life in the ministry. We knew as children that whenever the phone rang and a parishioner was calling for him, whether during mealtime or in the middle of the night, Dad was available, no questions asked. I have a clock on my mantle that was given to my dad by a family whose teenage son was suddenly stricken with a seizure and diagnosed with an advanced, malignant brain tumor. The boy's father was an antique dealer and my father was with that family for several weeks. I must have been only seven or eight years old, but I vividly remember Dad saying he was going to the Hansen home again, or to the hospital to be with the Hansens. That family let my father share in every moment of the last days of their son's life, and entrusted Dad to be there, to lead a prayer, sometimes just to sit in silence with the family, eventually to be with them and Billy when his life support was disconnected. After Billy's death, they brought an ornate, antique mantle clock to our home and gave it to my father as a gift of thanks. They grieved the devastating loss of their child, but not as a people without hope.

What the Hansen family will never know is that my little patients who come to therapy in my home office have learned to listen with their hearing aids or cochlear implants, thanks to that very same clock because it strikes on the hour and half-hour, with a low-pitch, loud, almost authoritative sound. Over the past ten years, countless children with hearing loss who are just learning to listen and to identify the sounds in their world have heard and recognized that clock striking, pointing to their ear, saying "Listen!" while a mother or father relishes this small victory in learning. Sometimes when it strikes, I am reminded of what that clock represents in the cycle of re-creation, in the relationship between a dying boy, his parents, and the pastor who cared for them through great loss, grieving and ultimately, hope. This is such a poignant story for me because it speaks strongly of the two greatest events of our lives, birth and death. The parents of Billy Hansen gave up their son to the keeping of the heavenly Father. But in his death Billy gave the gift of discovery, wonder, learning, and the excitement of an experience to a whole new generation of children. This clock will go on striking for new generations of children with hearing loss to hear for the first time and to exclaim, no doubt, "Listen!"

## Thin Places

WHAT DAD SHARED WITH THE HANSENS, AND WITH SO MANY OTHERS during his ministry was, as the Celts called it, a "thin place." That is, a time so intimate, when the veil between the material and the spiritual world is so thin that one can see and almost touch the other world. I shall always be grateful to Dr. John Niparko, George T. Nager Professor of Otolaryngology – Head and Neck Surgery at the Johns Hopkins University School of Medicine, who first described this concept of "thin places" to me. I encourage those interested to read about this fascinating concept of the spirit world. After John shared with me a keynote address on this topic that had been given by Rev. James

Miller in 2000 at the American Academy of Otolaryngology-Head & Neck Surgery, I finally had an adequate descriptor for the phenomenon I had sometimes experienced in my personal life. But I also recognized that I had experienced this in my clinical practice, if only occasionally and briefly, and that it was this phenomenon that transformed my vocation from a "strong interest" to a vocation that I now see as "a divine summons." And this is how, after all these years, Dad's vocation and mine have so perfectly intersected. We, like so many of you my colleagues, find deep satisfaction and a connection to something greater than the moment, within the rare but profound thin places of relationships.

## Cycles and Circles Again

THE CELTS AND THEIR THIN PLACES TAKE US BACK TO THE NOTION OF CYCLES and circles that began this First Day's entry. Anyone who has admired Celtic art forms, whether viewing the magnificent Book of Kells, that glorious illuminated manuscript in Dublin, or owning a piece of Celtic-style jewelry, knows the theme of circles, loops and intertwining spirals that characterize this style of art. Theologian Rosemary Haughton reminds us that, "The spiral is the symbol of a centeredness that doesn't look up or down or keep heaven and earth separate, but looks both within and without and finds the divine in mountain and well and horses and human heroism and love, and isn't quite sure where the divine ends and the human begins."

Like the spiral, there is the labyrinth and the mandala. On the cover of this book is a Celtic Mandala, created by Elantu Veovode whom I met at the North American Scottish festival in Estes Park, Colorado. From our first conversation, I sensed in Elantu a special talent and spirit, and she has taught me how the Celts' philosophy is reflected in their artwork. Elantu has written that, "This artwork represents the inextricable bonds of interdependence of living things upon each other. Flowers, birds, animals and humans are entwined in a mandala, held together by woven cords such that, if one connection is changed, then all the others must change in order to maintain balance." These features, for the Celts, represented the reverence for eternal life and the interconnection of everything and every person, much like the symbol of the circle described at the beginning of this chapter. Knowing this, it seemed that Elantu's Celtic Mandala was meant for the cover of this book.

## Vocation Revisited

WHAT I STILL SOMETIMES STRUGGLE WITH, AND I KNOW OTHERS DO TOO, IS the difference between my work being a job and it being a vocation. "My work (teaching) is more than dry labor; it is virtue spiced by passion, it is a tantalizing main course set before me daily. It ensures that I do not live my life, in Mary Oliver's words, 'simply having visited this world'. " (Marianne Novak, from *Living the Questions*, p. 28).

Have you tasted a "tantalizing main course" in your work with special-needs children? I know I have. Not every day, or with every patient, but occasionally, that experience of tasting work "spiced by passion," feeds me, sustains my commitment to my vocation. In contrast, there have been times when I have felt I just have a job that makes me a living or provides some security. During those times, I hunger for more, I feel the need for sustenance that will challenge my mind and feed my soul. It is only when I remind myself that the work I do for children and families is a vocation that involves my dedication to God as the source of that work that I am renewed in purpose and strength. Dr. William Placher of Wabash College, on the very first page of his marvelous book, *Callings*, reminds me of a quote from Dag Hammarskjold: "I don't know Who - or what - put the question, I don't know when it was put. I don't even remember answering. But at some moment I did answer, Yes to Someone - or Something - and from that hour I was certain that existence is meaningful and that, therefore, my life, in self-surrender, had a goal." Day by day, for me, that self-surrender is to God for making my life count and making my vocation an instrument of God's love for people.

*So this first day of Creation ends with the promise of John's Gospel, "I am the Light of the world, whoever follows me will never walk in darkness but will have the Light of life." I am apt to remember too, "The Light shines in the darkness and the darkness has never overcome it." (John 1:5) Thank you, Creator God, for light everywhere. Shine, shine, for everyone, wherever children endure and parents give praise for even small victories.*

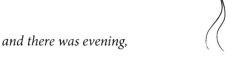

*I close my journal with,*

*"And there was morning and there was evening, the first day."*

# RESOURCES FOR
# RE-CREATION OF VOCATIONAL COMMITMENT

## Individual Resources

1. Read all or parts of some of the marvelous books on vocational renewal, even if you, like me, have time to read only one chapter or section at a time. Consider: *Let Your Life Speak – Listening for the Voice of Vocation* by Parker Palmer; *Leading Lives that Matter – What We Should Do and Who We Should Be* edited by Schwehn and Bass; Dave Sindrey introduced me to the inspiring book, *To Be of Use – the Seven Seeds of Meaningful Work* by Dave Smith, the cofounder of Smith & Hawken company.

2. Poetry is a resource that inspires and challenges us. At the top of my recommended list is *Teaching With Fire – Poetry that Sustains the Courage to Teach* edited by Intrator and Scribner, a masterful collection of submitted poems and what each poem has meant to a teacher. *Poems to Read: A New Favorite Poem Project Anthology* edited by Pinsky and Dietz are poems meant to be read aloud, also with commentary by those who submitted their favorite poems.

3. Keep small "words of wisdom" cards near your desk at work and change them often. Maintain a gratitude file – notes of thanks and appreciation sent by parents or colleagues, pictures expressing love drawn by your patients. Take the file out at times when vocational commitment is waning and read through these notes. Be reminded of the ways in which your work has touched others, your vocational summons has made a difference to children and their families.

4. Meditate, contemplate, pray or practice mindfulness as you are comfortable to find inspiration for new life, new creation, in your vocational calling. *Pocket Prayers* collected by June Cotner, are 36 small cards with some lovely prayers for all faiths.

5. Another source I have gone to when my vocational commitment falters is *Laughter, Silence and Shouting – An anthology of Women's Prayers* edited by Kathy Keay. I have prayed the following prayer many times, sometimes in celebration, sometimes in frustration.

> *Work*
>
> *That which I give my energy to;*
> *which I love*
> *hate*
> *find challenging*
> *demanding*
> *frustrating*
> *rewarding:*

*This is my work –*
*that which I must do*
*on a daily basis*
*In order to live*
*and to prove*
*that I am fully alive.*

*Lord, thank you that as we work in the world*
*engaging our best energies*
*in that which is before us,*
*you work within us*
*through that same struggle,*
*the fabric of our redemption.*
*-Kathy Keay*

# Group Resources

1. A group member might review one of the stories of vocational commitment found in *The Power of Purpose – Creating Meaning in your Life and Work* by Richard Leider; *The Life of Meaning* by Abernethy and Bole; or *Leading Lives that Matter – What We Should Do and Who We Should Be* edited by Schwehn and Bass. How does the experience of another person's vocational quest impact your own story?

2. Select someone to read aloud a poem and the accompanying commentary from *Teaching With Fire – Poetry that Sustains the Courage to Teach*. Each poem was submitted by a teacher with a short explanation of what that poem has meant in his or her vocational calling. Not infrequently, I hear in my mind this question from Mary Oliver's poem, "The Summer Day", "Tell me, what is it you plan to do with your one wild and precious life?" Share with the group how that poem affects you and add other selections to be read aloud and pondered.

3. The Celts used the term "Thin Places" to describe the most intimate and spiritual moments in one's life. At what times in your career, if any, can you say you touched a thin place in your relationship with a patient or family?

4. Recall a moment in your vocational life when you felt you were doing exactly what you were called to do. Complete the sentence, "I felt I was where I was meant to be when_____." How do others in the group complete this sentence? Is there a thread that seems to weave across the experiences of those who respond? Are group members' experiences different from each others'?

# THE SECOND DAY

# RE-CREATION AFTER DISCOURAGEMENT

*And God said, "Let there be a firmament in the midst of the waters, and let it separate the waters from the waters...." (Gen.1:6)*

*The water that I give them shall be a perpetual spring within them, giving them eternal life. (John 4:14)*

*Turn Over Gently*

*Turn over*
*Gently*
*My dry, cracked soil.*
*Just a little,*
*A little at a time.*
*Let it breathe*
*In the cooling air of autumn*
*And then be watered*
*By your life-giving rain.*
                    *-Kathy Keay*

# Water, Water Everywhere

*In my own way as a human being with strengths and weaknesses, Jesus as the Water of Life quenches my thirst and cleanses me. I haven't always been crazy about that cleansing part because it acknowledges my imperfections - but that's in the mix too. Parker Palmer writes that, "If I let my life speak things I want to hear, I must also let it speak things I do not want to hear and would never tell anyone. My life is not only about my strengths and virtues, it is also about my liabilities and my limitations." Yet, acknowledging these is truthful, liberating, and leads, ultimately, to being what we are meant to be. So, I have come to see that part of the renewal of my vocation and my faith may be listening to a piece of music or taking a hot bath when I'm fatigued out of my mind. Water for me, is a balm that can rinse away the mistakes, the impurities of the day. I read the 23d Psalm with its "green pastures and beside still waters" and find myself caught up in the appeal of water as the symbol of restoration.*

IN GOING THROUGH MY JOURNAL NOTES FOR THIS SECOND DAY OF CREATION IT occurs to me that there is probably none of us who cannot conjure up memories of water from childhood. Didn't we all wade in muddy ditches after a downpour, dive endlessly into swimming pools, paddle a canoe, look for those elusive fish in the lake? Didn't we enjoy a hot bath on a cold day, appreciate the abundance of water everywhere around us? After all, we spent the first nine months of our lives in water. What surpasses the delight of a cold glass of lemonade on a hot afternoon? Living my teenage years in Panama on the Pacific Ocean, many Saturdays were spent at a beach called Rio Mar, where a fresh-water river met the ocean with its formidable waves for surfing (I left that to my friends who had grown up on the ocean) so you had your pick of the salty ocean or a dip in the sweet river water.

When I think of the work ahead of me on this second day of Re-creation, looking over the tasks on my "to do" list, I can't help but contrast those to the tasks my father would have had on his "to do" list as the pastor of a congregation. If I am sometimes moved, even overwhelmed by the emotional aspects of my work with children and families, what must it be like for a pastor to have a "to do" list that reads: "Perform Mary's funeral; visit Paul in hospice center; baptize Esther in Pacific Ocean." The last item was a joyful task that I remember well. It happened on Easter Sunday morning in the early 1970's when members of our Balboa congregation gathered at sunrise along the shore of the Pacific Ocean to celebrate the resurrection. One of the special moments came when my father led an elderly woman out into the water for her baptism, something she had requested. My father in t-shirt and cutoff jeans and Esther in her long gown stood in the rising sunlight, the water washing against them, the whole Pacific Ocean a backdrop like a painting by Gauguin. My father gently dipped dear Esther forward three times and in that vast ocean they embraced in faith and jubilation as living witness to the promise of Jesus, "Where two or three are gathered together, there am I in the midst of them." Water is, and has been from the beginning of time, the necessary ingredient for all life. No wonder God made water so early in his Creation. Did the writer of the Creation story know something it took science a lot longer to learn, that water was the habitat in which all life began?

## Vocational Drought

THE LACK OF WATER CAN ALSO BRING DROUGHT. ABSENCE OF WATER IS DEVAS-tating to farmers, fatal to those who live in water-deprived deserts when the rains don't come. Much of the Middle East was so water-deprived in biblical times, as now of course that the Bible writers referred often to the vitality, precious-ness and symbolism of water. Most of us in the United States have little appreciation for what water must have meant to our biblical forbearers. It was used by Jesus as the eternally hopeful symbol of new life through baptism, even of hospitality in offering to wash the feet of one's house guest after a long journey.

I have experienced many periods of vocational drought over the years – times when I felt dry and parched – waterless – like an empty well.  Probably the most common time I feel parchedness is when I am tired – and that's not infrequently! Does anyone in our profession get enough sleep? Most of us start our work early in the morning. It's common for surgeons to report to the operating room at 6 a.m. Audiologists and therapists often come early for 7 a.m. meetings, and work until 5:00 or later. During IEP time, I have known teachers who had 7 a.m. case conferences every morning for two weeks solid, then had to rush off to class, teach a full day, and then perhaps even have more conferences after school.  Evenings are spent correcting homework, grading papers, preparing therapy materials for the next day, not to mention tending to family, spouse, and self.

I know I'm writing primarily to my colleagues in the field of special needs children, but this lesson is no less relevant for those in other professions. Does anyone know, for example, how many hours a farmer works in a week? Congregations would be appalled if they knew what a schedule of seven days a week, 24 hours a day costs a pastor in personal and family time. Soldiers in battle often know nothing of sound sleep or mental and physical rest. Long hours and hard work is endemic all across the spectrum of human society.

For me, fatigue dries out my soul as nothing else. I can still go through the motions of the day, see my patients, return phone calls, but I feel empty and listless. And what about the related, equally draining feeling of being isolated or perceiving that we are away from our colleagues, maybe doing it all alone? Sometimes like the Psalmist, "I am like a lonely bird on the housetop" (Ps.102:7).

A second dryness of the soul are the times I just lose heart with the work I'm doing. Let's face it: caring for children who have special needs is tough work. Working with their families is tough work. Fulfilling, yes, but tough, all the same. Parker Palmer (*Courage to Teach Guide*, 2007, p. viii) reminds us that any field that attracts people for "reasons of the heart," risks those people suffering from losing heart. "How can we take heart again," we might ask ourselves, "so that we can give heart to others?" As Palmer notes, this is why we went into the profession to begin with.

The third dryness of the soul I experience is disappointment, especially at not being able to help a child or family the way I had hoped. I think of how we in the serving professions deal with disappointment, despair – not the small frustrations of each day (now where did I put the toys from that therapy kit?) but the regret and sense of futility that may come when we feel we have failed. It is an inevitable part of our work; we can't help everyone the way we'd like, some children don't respond to treatment even when we've done our best. I have felt sadness when I have given bad news to a family. One family, in particular, I had grown close to through parent-infant therapy. The test results on their two year old daughter, Katherine, born with normal hearing but deafened from a bacterial infection at five months showed that her second cochlear implant, like the first, had failed to stimulate any hearing and there was nothing else that could be done to help her hear.

## Grief and the Parched Soul

THE DAY MY MOTHER DIED IN 1973 AT THE AGE OF 44 WAS A TIME OF DEEP sadness in our family. My sisters and I lived with our parents in Balboa, Panama, but this was just about to change when our mother died. Celia and I would be returning to the US soon, she to finish her college career, I to begin mine. My brother Joel was home on emergency leave from military service. The sense of loss in our family was to such a great extent based upon our knowledge that our family was breaking up. My father and 12-year old sister, Anne, would remain in our home in Panama but the other three of us would soon scatter. It is hard for me now to describe those feelings, but I think of all the things that ever caused me grief the most poignant was the sense of our family losing its cohesion. Each time I would return home from college in Virginia, or later from my work, I would feel the absence of my mother who, along with my father, formed the nucleus of our family. My mother was a person of great faith and her influence on all of us has continued to this day. I guess her death was a pure echo of that biblical cry, "Why are you cast down, O my soul!"

I now see how "things work together for those who love the Lord" (Rom. 8:28). I remember those long midnight talks with my mother during her illness. These are precious to me. I remember how the congregation of Balboa Union Church brought into our home every night for months and months a complete dinner for our family, so many families having a part in that. I remember my father saying to Anne, "Anne, you and I are a smaller family now but still the same family, just smaller." I think when all the ingredients of my mother's life, death, and the history of our family afterwards are all put together into a whole, I see the "thread of gold" that the poet Jean Ingelow wrote in her poem, "Sorrows Humanize Our Race."

> For life is one, and in its warp and woof
> There runs a thread of gold that glitters fair,
> And sometimes in the pattern shows more sweet
> Where there are somber colors.  It is true
> That we have wept.  But O, this thread of gold,
> We would not have it tarnish……..

My mother's death at age 44 represents the deepest grief, the most somber colors in the tapestry of my life. No poet is going to convince me otherwise. There is that thread of gold, though, her immortal spirit I have sensed around me often in the years since she died – and as Anne Lamott writes in *Traveling Mercies*, there are big pieces of my mother still inside me, and I want those pieces in me for the rest of my life. Even when they bring sadness or even, sometimes still, deep sorrow.

## Watering the Parched Soul

I HAVE BEEN DRAWN TO THREE RESOURCES IN MOMENTS OF DESPAIR -MUSIC, THE writings of authors who have experienced and described their overcoming of despair and depression, and the book of Psalms. During the winter of my clinical fellowship year at Boys Town Hospital I came down with a hideous case of the flu. In my apartment, I medicated myself on everything I could think of that might cure the flu and went to bed for what turned out to be several days. On Sunday morning, still sick, I turned on my little radio to try to break the monotony of being in bed. I don't remember everything about that morning except through the fog of stopped up ears I heard music. I felt lonely, physically sick, inadequate as a first-year clinician working among experienced and well-known colleagues. Suddenly I heard a song that was so simple and so haunting that it ran through my head over and over again during those days when I was recovering, and it had such personal meaning for me. It was George Harrison, whose lyrics deal often with sacred and mystical themes, warning me in, "Beware of Darkness" (*All Things Must Pass* album) to "Watch out now, take care, beware of thoughts that linger, winding up inside your head." Harrison went on to sing of a sense of despair that may visit you, a "…hopelessness around you in the dead of night." I know others have had the experience of sensing that a piece of music was addressed to them personally, and that is how I felt as I listened on: "Beware of sadness," he sang. "It can hit you, it can hurt you - make you sore and what is more that is not what you are here for."

That is not what I am here for? Wow, I had to think about that for a while. Okay, God, what AM I here for? Nothing has helped me explore this question – not answer it – but explore it, more meaningfully than the writings of Parker Palmer. When I read, *Let Your Life Speak: Listening for the Voice of Vocation* I became aware of Palmer's spin on the notion of vocation. He suggests we ask ourselves, "Is the life I am living same life that wants to live in me?" The still, small voice I write about often in my journal emerges again, because the word "vocation" has the Latin word for "voice" at its root. But, Palmer doesn't suggest there is a voice calling from outside myself, as in, "Hey, Amy, this is what you're here for," but rather, a voice inside myself, calling me, as Palmer writes, "…to be the person I was born to be; to fulfill the original selfhood given by God at my birth." (p. 10). In short, vocation is a gift to be accepted graciously.

So, I still struggle with George Harrison's, "…that is not what you are here for." But, it is a bit clearer than before. We are here, it seems to me, to show faithfulness to those values that define us. We give ourselves names, identities. We call ourselves Christian, Jewish, Muslim, Catholic, Presbyterian, father, mother, therapist. Within each identity is a set of values that guides, challenges, and even corrects us. I don't think I am here for the purpose of having my name in the professional bright lights but rather for the purpose of being faithful to who I am and what I was born to be. I can see now that most of the times of sadness I feel in my life come from knowing I have fallen short in this faithfulness. In those sad periods, I realize that I have faltered in my faith, family life or professional duties, with a patient or a friend - in some way in each of these instances I have failed to remain true to the values that identify me. I have come to believe that I am in this faith, this family, and this profession to be a blessing to God who is more than Christian, Jewish or Muslim, who is, in fact, over all. One of the prayers I pray from the Psalms clarifies both my purpose and God's place in that purpose:

*Let the words of my mouth and the meditation of my heart*
*Be acceptable in thy sight, O Lord, my Guide and Redeemer.*
*Ps.19:14*

Harrison, a deeply spiritual person, was drawn to the Eastern, Hindu traditions. Two thousand years earlier, the Psalmist expressed a similar theme about the hopelessness that can surround us, in the dead of night.

### Psalm 64

*O You who hear all hearts, hear my plea;*
*Preserve my life when fears beset me*
*When doubts rise up and leave me trembling;*
*As powerful as arrows they strike the heart,*
*Building armored walls that keep Love at bay*
*murmuring secretly in the darkness,*
*"Who can see us?"*

*Water and faith are showing up everywhere! I read in my devotions today something Shakespeare wrote, "Smooth runs the water when the brook runs deep" (II Henry VI). I can find few definitions of a religious faith truer than that. As I kneel in prayer, I have before me a Grandparent's book that Dad wrote in for my boys when they were little. It is almost sacred to me, as some of his entries in it are priceless, such as this one: "When I was seven or eight, I went with my Sunday School class to a picnic along a river in Kansas. My teacher took us on a kind of nature hike. He showed us the shallow water flowing over the rocks in the river bed. 'If this water flows over these stones long enough," he said, "the stones will disappear.' I couldn't believe that or understand it then. But I've always remembered it as a great lesson in patience and endurance." Then out of the blue, my oldest son, Campbell, an English and Religion major at college, handed me a book last night of texts from the Daoist faith tradition, written by the Daoist sage, Lao Tzu. He showed me a certain spot he'd been reading about a central concept of Daoism, "wu-wei", meaning "action without force." Campbell noted that wu-wei is associated with water through its yielding nature. At first glance, water is soft and weak, the text said, but it can move earth and carve stone. So it is that, 75 years later, Campbell is intrigued by a concept his grandfather had experienced generations earlier and had preserved for him in his Sunday School story. I say a prayer of thankfulness for the presence of wise and loving grandparents everywhere.*

# Discouragement in Far-Away Places

HOW FORTUNATE I HAVE BEEN IN MY WORK TO TRAVEL EXTENSIVELY TO observe the dedicated clinicians working around the world, in settings similar to, and vastly different from, my own. I watch therapists putting in long hours everywhere, on behalf of children with special needs. Sitting in on therapy sessions for deaf children with cochlear implants in Seoul, Korea, Bogotá, Colombia, or Ankara, Turkey brings a thrill, a renewed hope, a sensation like the warm waters of the Caribbean.

The flip side is that travel is exhausting, it takes us away from our families, and it can bring deep discouragement. Some of the greatest discouragement I have ever felt was teaching in Beijing, China. It was thrilling to be there, but the magnitude of the problems of deaf education were mind-boggling. The sheer number of children with hearing loss in that country is hard to fathom (some estimates are that 21 million children in China are born deaf and another 66 million will lose hearing during their lifetime.) This is not even considering the severe shortage of available resources to serve these children. At moments such as these, the tension of standing in the tragic gap between what we know is possible and what we see is reality was as acute as it has ever been for me. How tempting to become pessimistic, even cynical, about the enormity of the challenge and one's inability to make any difference at all. I have spoken with many colleagues who have experienced similar feelings when traveling abroad. Not only do you see the devastating scale of the problem, you wonder what could possibly be done to even begin making things better for the children there. On top of that, you feel exhausted, almost smothered by the well-meaning clinicians who tend to bombard you. They want so much to just ask one question, to get advice on a patient of theirs with a special problem. You try, but you may feel close to being drained absolutely dry.

I taught for three days at Peking University in an unventilated classroom with desks for only 20 students, but packed with 60 people, sitting on the floor, on the window sills, leaning against the walls. They wanted so much to learn, yet their lack of basic knowledge was discouraging and the range of questions left my head spinning with uncertainty. How to even begin to address their urgent needs?

At the end of the first day in Beijing, I went back to my hotel and prayed, "Father, give me wisdom to offer one or two things that will benefit these teachers tomorrow. I know I cannot solve their problems completely. But, how can I make a difference, even a small difference, for one child?" Then I was reminded of the story of the huge group of starfish that had beached up on the shore. Thousands of starfish that would dry out in the sun and die. A man watched as a small boy slowly picked up a single starfish, walked back to the water and threw it in. "Son," the man said, "you might as well not even try doing that. It was very kind of you, but don't you see that what you just did, it's not going to make a difference for all these starfish." The boy answered confidently, "Well, it made a difference for that one." My hope is that the following day when I taught in that classroom in Beijing, I was able to make a difference for at least one teacher who made a difference for at least one child.

## *Providing for Others When we are Drained*

IN ANOTHER INCIDENT AFTER A LONG DAY OF SPEAKING IN SANTIAGO, CHILE, I was getting into my hostess's car to be driven back to my hotel for a much-needed nap before our 10:30 p.m. dinner. (My years of growing up in Panama partially prepared me for this Latin custom of late meals and late nights, but it's getting harder as I grow, well… older.) A therapist from the conference approached our car. She had a video clip of a patient of hers on her laptop, she said excitedly. I tried to explain as politely as I could that I really had to be leaving, but she persisted. Would I please allow her to sit next to me with two other people in the back seat of a car the size of an Austin Mini? She offered to hold the computer on her lap as we crossed the city to my hotel so I could watch the video and tell her what she should be doing differently in her therapy to more effectively teach this child who had received a cochlear implant. I had no resistance left in me. Yes, I would watch, I answered, and so we rode across the city, watching the video of a congenitally-deaf child who could now talk and sing, thanks to a cochlear implant, her parents, and the fierce dedication of a clinician who wouldn't give up on one little starfish.

The next morning, my hosts were kind enough to take me to beautiful Viña del Mar, right on the coast. Talk about spiritual renewal and the healing power of water! I looked out on the vast Pacific Ocean, I thought of the prayer by Carla Piette, a Chilean poet and Maryknoll nun*:

### Waters of God

*Waters of mountains, waters of God*
*Cleanse us, renew us, so shabbily shod*
*Rios de Chile, streams of burnt snow*
*Melt us, toe us beyond friend or foe.*
*Currents so fast, pools deep and clear*
*Tune us, quiet our hearts still to hear.*
*Lord of the River, God of the Stream*
*Teach us Your song, our dryness redeem.*
　　　*-Carla Piette*

**\*Carla Piette left Chile to work in El Salvador following the assassination of Archbishop Oscar Romero there. She drowned in an over-turned jeep while helping Sister Ita Ford rescue a political prisoner in the Salvadoran mountains in August, 1980. Three months later, Sr. Ita Ford and three other Catholic missionaries were tortured, raped and murdered by Salvadoran soldiers.**

I GAZED OUT ON THOSE "WATERS OF GOD" THAT SUNNY SATURDAY, SERENE, CON-
tent, enthusiastic, and it was hard to believe that less than 24 hours earlier I had
felt depleted of energy, empty of ideas. The power of water at work! Blessed
water. I thought of that masterpiece of a novel, *Gilead*, by Marilynne Robinson,
about an aged, dying minister who writes down his life lessons for his young son.
In one scene, the minister reminisces about himself and his young bride laughing
and running while getting drenched in a downpour. The elderly man ponders, "It
is easy to believe in such moments that water was made primarily for blessing, and
only secondarily for growing vegetables or doing the wash. I wish I had paid more
attention to it" (p. 28).

## *The Buoyancy of Water and the Spirit*

C RAIG DYKSTRA, A LEADING THEOLOGIAN AND SENIOR VICE-PRESIDENT FOR
Religion at the Lilly Endowment has written a recent essay, "Pastoral and
Ecclesial Imagination." I believe this essay relates perfectly to our experience
of knowing that, in our spirituality, we experience a connectedness with more than
the concrete events of the day. Craig writes of his days in college, earning money by
giving swimming lessons to preschoolers, gently introducing them to the feel of the
water, all the while supporting them so that they would not go under or sink into
the water. Gradually, as the children adjusted and became comfortable with the feel
of the water, they realized something profound and surprising: that the water was
buoyant – they did not have to struggle and do all the work to keep from sinking.
The water had a quality that buoyed them so that they were, in fact, almost weight-
less in it, and Craig watched as each child became free to enjoy the pool because
they were bourn up by the buoyancy of the water. Craig writes: "The first priority
in teaching children to swim is to enable them to trust the water. Somehow or another they have to come to a specific kind of knowledge..... It is not something you
can teach children – or anyone else, for that matter – through a lesson in physics.
Objective as it is, for the sake of swimming one has to come to know it personally."

"So it is with the life of faith," Dykstra continues. "At the heart of the Christian
life there lies a deep, somatic, profoundly personal but very real knowledge. It is
the knowledge of the buoyancy of God. It is the knowledge that in struggle and in
joy, in conflict and in peace, indeed, in every possible circumstance and condition
of life and in death – we are upheld by God's own everlasting arms" (p. 55). For
me personally this means that I do not have to take on the struggle all by myself. I
do not have to fight for my life to stay afloat when fear, doubt, disappointment or
discouragement confront me. The buoyancy of my faith is there to keep me from
sinking.

# Buoyancy in the Face of Despair

*I need some of that buoyancy now, feeling discouraged after working for months with a family to set up an appropriate program in a school district for their three-year old son who has multiple disabilities. The district failed to provide even the minimal standard of education, and the parents, a state advocate, and I formulated a plan that could meet his needs. During the case conference on this child, my heart sank when the parents simply could not find it within themselves to tolerate the level of conflict that it would take to secure adequate services for their child, and ended up agreeing to the inadequate and inappropriate program the school district proposed. I couldn't sleep that night, thinking of the unfairness, of the lost opportunity for this child, for the well-meaning parents who didn't have the courage to face a hostile school administrator. I remembered Eckart Tolle's suggestion from his book, The Power of Now, that when our mind focuses or obsesses on things, especially negative ones, we should become the watcher of the thoughts, identifying them and naming the emotion but trying not to become that emotion. As I lay in bed, I acknowledged, "Disappointment is here" rather than, "I am disappointed" or "Those parents disappointed me" or "That school district disappointed me." It sounds like just a trick of semantic word play, but I was surprised that it created a subtle but forceful change and allowed me to fall asleep.*

Throughout this discouraging experience, I thought of the poem Craig Dykstra uses in *Leading from Within* that relates to his theme of the buoyancy of God. Hearing this poem in my head gave me a sense of that buoyancy and reassurance that I was not in this situation alone.

### The Avowal

> *As swimmers dare*
> *to lie face to the sky*
> *and water bears them,*
> *as hawks rest upon air*
> *and air sustains them,*
> *so would I learn to attain*
> *freefall, and float*
> *into Creator Spirit's deep embrace,*
> *knowing no effort earns*
> *that all-surrounding grace.*
>            *-Denise Levertov*

# Water and Communication Disorders

I JUST COULD NOT PUT DOWN ON PAPER THOUGHTS ABOUT THIS SECOND DAY of Creation with its emphasis on the life-giving gift of water without sharing a journal entry from the early days of my marriage to Clay. Soon after our marriage Clay and I moved to Brussels, Belgium, settled into a seventh-floor apartment and bought an old baby-blue Citroen Deux Chevaux car that ran some of the time. The first few weeks and months were often discouraging, even as excited as we had been about moving there. Every little thing that would come effortlessly in the U.S. took energy and time, and doing and re-doing, largely because my French proficiency was so limited. Coincidentally, a story about water illustrates my frustrations and misunderstandings during those early months.

One day, just after arriving, the intercom sounded from the street level. "Madame?" a male voice said, as he began a rapid and lengthy explanation in French. I hesitated, trying to decipher any bits of the message I had just heard. Understanding a foreign language is difficult enough face-to-face, but particularly challenging over the telephone because you can't see the speaker's face, gestures or expressions, all of which aid comprehension. Hadn't I told many parents of deaf children this very thing over the years? I was now a living example of it. Trying desperately to fill in my gaps in understanding, I processed the words "trente minutes" and "l'eau", and took this to mean that something was going to take place in thirty minutes that had to do with water. Suddenly I understood, based upon an event from the first week we had lived there. He was telling the residents that the water was going to be shut off in 30 minutes, assuming that people would want to store some for making dinner. "Thank you, Sir...merci, Monsieur –...I understand!"

I had a truly satisfying feeling as I filled the kitchen sink and some pans with water. Things were getting easier there, I had to admit. My French was really improving, thanks to the classes Clay and I were taking. I would have called Clay at his office to tell him of my little victory, but it would be another six weeks before we had phone service! I celebrated my linguistic progress with an afternoon nap.

A few hours later, I tried the water for the first time. Sure enough, it had been turned back on so I started dinner, eagerly awaiting Clay's arrival home from work. I looked down from our large apartment windows and what I saw on the street below took me a moment to process. The street, normally lined solid with parked cars on both sides, was completely empty of vehicles – with one exception. My baby-blue Deux Chevaux was parked on the street all by itself. Every inch of it was splattered with mud, streaks of dirt and other debris. The street was spotlessly clean otherwise, with puddles of water still drying in some spots. It suddenly became clear to me what the man had tried to tell me: that all the residents should move their cars within thirty minutes because the street cleaning trucks would be coming through to power-spray with water! I should have laughed it off, and I do laugh about it now, but at the time, I felt like crying. If ever I felt empathy for children with communication disorders, it was during that year because I was, without a doubt, a seriously communicatively-impaired person. I was also a stranger in a strange country, and that made me feel as though I were wandering in desert places, or a prisoner of affliction, or lost at sea in a terrible storm.

## Back to the Psalms

*I refer back to the Psalms a lot in my journal but that's because they are an unending source of spiritual inspiration and comfort for me. Often, especially in these early morning times when I look out this little window and imagine I'm an observer at the Creation, it is the Psalms I read, make notes about, and remember far beyond these early morning devotions.*

ONE OCTOBER SUNDAY MORNING, AFTER MY EXPERIENCE WITH THE STREET cleaners, the pastor of our church in Brussels gave his sermon based on Psalm 107. This Psalm was probably composed originally as a kind of antiphonal celebration of God's mercies conducted between a leader and the congregation.

The Pastor read from the Psalm:

Some wandered in desert wastes, finding no city to dwell in, hungry and thirsty, their soul fainted within them. Then they cried to the Lord in their trouble and he delivered them from their distress.

From the congregation we responded:

Let us thank the Lord for his steadfast love, for his wonderful works to the sons and daughters of men.

Pastor:

Some sat in darkness and gloom, prisoners in affliction. Their hearts were bowed down with hard labor, they fell down, with none to help. Then they cried to the Lord in their trouble and he delivered them from their distress.

Congregation:

Let us thank the Lord for his steadfast love, for his wonderful works to the sons and daughters of men.

The Pastor and congregation continued together through Psalm 107. Somehow the way it was done, antiphonally, made me understand more fully the disappointment I had experienced when I felt I was wandering in desert places or was a prisoner of affliction, a person lost at sea in a terrible storm. I identified with my deep belief that while God is no Magic Man pulling rabbits out of a hat, faith for me is a power of the spirit and that it can, and does, save and inspire.

## Undeserved Showers of Blessing

JUST AS I ACKNOWLEDGE TIMES OF DISAPPOINTMENT AND DISCOURAGEMENT, I must also admit that, at times, rejuvenation comes to me undeservedly and unexpectedly. I may wake up some morning feeling positively euphoric about my day, about the children and parents I'll see. In my childhood Sunday School classes we sang, "There shall be Showers of Blessing." Where does this unexplained "shower of blessing" come from? Henry W. Longfellow must have had an inkling when he wrote the following poem:

### As Torrents in Summer

*As torrents in summer*
*Half-dried in their channels,*
*Suddenly rise, though the*
*Sky is still cloudless,*
*For rain has been falling far off at their fountains.*

*So hearts that are fainting*
*Grow full to o'er flowing*
*And they that behold it marvel,*
*and know not*
*That God at their fountains*
*Far off has been raining!*
*-Henry W. Longfellow*

The waters of renewal, even in the face of discouragement, are flowing from a source deep and wide and one I sometimes perceive as being far, far away, like the "far off fountains" of the poem. But they are not. I just may be unaware of their presence, and of their source.

## Water and a Small Voice

I THINK OF WATER, ITS HEALING AND REJUVENATING EFFECTS, AND IT TAKES me back to Katharine. What a humbling lesson it has been for me to watch the development of this little girl who was unable to hear with either of her two cochlear implants. Admittedly, the parents and I were devastated when that news came. But, these wise and loving parents accepted Katharine just as she was and have loved her unconditionally, all of her – her beautiful blonde hair, her deafness, her devotion to her older brother, even her stubbornness. At the same time, they have high expectations for her, want her to develop as much speech as possible to augment her rapidly-improving sign language, and she is rising to their expectations. Several months after learning the disappointing news of her failed hearing, Katharine had still never spoken a truly intelligible word. Then one day, she and her mother came to therapy. "She said her first real word!" her mother announced excitedly. "It happened when I was running the water for her bath." From behind her back, Katharine produced a photograph of herself in a bathtub that was absolutely filled to the brim with bubbles. Only Katharine's sweet face peered upward, with bubbles all around her. "Bu-bu," she told me, laughing and pointing to the water and the bubbles. "Bu-bu!" A real word! As her mother had been running the water for the bath, Katharine gestured and signed for bubble bath to be added to the water, then she began saying, "Bu-bu", over and over. By all reports, this was followed by tears, laughter, hugs and the pouring of an entire bottle of bubble bath into the water. To celebrate this momentous occasion, her father had taken the picture of Katharine enveloped by her beloved bubbles.

I keep that photograph on my desk and depending on the moment, it conveys different meanings to me: sometimes when I look at it, I am reminded of the power of water; sometimes of a child's small voice and her first, magical spoken word; other times, of the devotion of parents everywhere to a child with special needs but an indomitable spirit.

*It is time to end my second day in this 7 day cycle of Creation. I put aside my Bible and my copy of "The Upper Room" and kneel for my prayer of departure. It is a prayer that I will be of use to the heavenly Father, his work of Creation, that I can be a partner through my profession and my faith in helping in ways given me to be a faithful witness to God. I thank Him for water and for all that water means in my life and in human life everywhere. This Sunday I hope the pastor of our church will have at least one baptism so I can say, maybe right out loud, "Let us thank the Lord for his steadfast love, for his wonderful works to the sons and daughters of men. Especially the children!"*

*I close my journal with, "And there was morning and there was evening, the second day."*

# RESOURCES FOR RE-CREATION AFTER DISCOURAGEMENT

## Individual Resources

1. Wherever you are, be present in the now. Read Eckart Tolle's book, *The Power of Now* and try the practice of describing emotions or states of mind as an observer, "Disappointment is here" rather than as a definition of self: "I am disappointed." Pema Chodron, an American Buddhist nun, writes in a similar vein of not letting our thoughts sweep us away. Just label them as "thinking," and try to let them go again (p. 21.)

2. Identify music that speaks to you, some of it uplifting, cheerful music; other selections soulful music that expresses how you feel, just as "Beware of Darkness" echoed my lingering painful thoughts.

3. If you are a person with a faith tradition, there may be hymns that are especially meaningful to you. Some that I am drawn to are "Wellspring of Wisdom" (M.T. Winter, 1987); and "When Our Confidence Is Shaken" (F.P. Green, 1971); and two of my favorites:

### O Love That Will Not Let Me Go

*"O Joy that seeketh me through pain,*
*I cannot close my heart to thee;*
*I trace the rainbow through the rain,*
*And feel the promise is not vain,*
*That morn shall tearless be."*
   *-G. Matheson, 1882 (stanza 3)*

### In Heavenly Love Abiding

*"In Heavenly love abiding, no change my heart shall fear*
*And safe in such confiding, for nothing changes here.*
*The storm may roar without me, my heart may low be laid;*
*But God is round about me, and can I be dismayed?"*
   *-Anna Laetitia Waring, 1850*

4. Give yourself permission to get away from your work – to take a break and focus on something very different from your profession, perhaps a hobby, or maybe even something mindless, like a comedy film that is just plain funny. No deep meaning there. I could watch "Planes, Trains and Automobiles" a hundred times and still laugh until it hurts when John Candy sings, "Do the Mess Around" while driving a rental car with the steering wheel between his knees. If I have been fret-

ting about something and then watch a movie like that, it's almost impossible to go back to the level of anguish that I felt beforehand. Who knew comedy could be one of God's healing balms?

5.  Keep a file in which you accumulate a storehouse of uplifting things related to your profession, colleagues, your students or patients. I have such a file, and one note in it was written by Paul, a 9-year old patient of mine who is bright, articulate, and dyslexic. I often have him practice writing essays, and one of his essays is priceless to me. I share it here with his permission, and also with the humble realization that this incredible, loving boy would probably single out any clinician who worked with him – I just happen to be the lucky one.

> "I have dyslexia. The name souns werde. I did not know wat it was up [at] first. But then my perens told mea. It rylly Bugs me to have dyslexia. But althow its annoying it has brot me grait things like to know ammy robins. I know allot about computers and to love ellectronixs. But now I know that great people have had dyslexia like Thomas Edeson, Albirt Inestine and allot of othor people. Alftor all, dyslexia is not all that bad!!!!!
>
> -Paul

## Group Resources

1. What practices do you rely on when you feel discouraged in your work? Do the effects of these practices ultimately have a positive or negative influence on your attitude or mood?

2. Share with others the music that speaks to you in times of discouragement. Do you gravitate toward uplifting, sing-along tunes, or melancholy music that expresses how you feel? Find the reggae DVD of hymns, "By the Rivers of Babylon", a compilation of different artists singing hymns in reggae style. Listen to the steel drum version of, "And there we wept, by the rivers of Babylon." It'll knock your socks off.

3. Respond to this question recently posed by Parker Palmer: "How do I stay close to the passions and commitments that took me into this work, challenging myself and my colleagues and the institution I work in to keep faith with this profession's deepest values?" (*Christian Century*, Oct. 2, 2007; 28-32)

4. As professionals, we often must measure our success one child at a time, much like the boy from the story who felt satisfaction rescuing a single starfish. Complete the sentence: "I made a real difference in one child's life when _____."

5. On the theme of water, use the following poem by William Stafford as a starting point for discussion about discouragement in your work. What is your "river of ice?" Where are "hidden currents" in your work?

*Ask Me*

*Some time when the river is ice ask me*
*mistakes I have made. Ask me whether*
*what I have done is my life. Others*
*have come in their slow way into*
*my thought, and some have tried to help*
*or to hurt: ask me what difference*
*their strongest love or hate has made.*

*I will listen to what you say.*
*You and I can turn and look*
*at the silent river and wait. We know*
*the current is there, hidden; and there*
*are comings and goings from miles away*
*that hold the stillness exactly before us.*
*What the river says, that is what I say.*

*-William Stafford*

# THE THIRD DAY

# RE-CREATION
# OF PERSONAL
# RELATIONSHIPS AND
# FAMILY LIFE

*God called the dry land earth...and God saw that it was good. Let the earth bring forth vegetation, plants...fruit trees in which is their seed, each according to their kind. (Gen.1:10)*

*For the Fruits of This Creation*

*For the harvests of the spirit, thanks be to God;*
*For the good we all inherit, thanks be to God;*
*For the wonders that astound us,*
*For the truths that still confound us;*
*Most of all, that love has found us,*
*Thanks be to God.*
                    *-Fred Pratt Green*

ON THIS THIRD DAY OF CREATION, MY JOURNAL REMINDS ME THAT THE BIBLI-cal concept of family begins as early as Chapter 4 of Genesis. In that spirit, and guided by that wisdom, I turn to my life's relationships, friends, loved ones, and especially family. I do this because all of us in this profession of helping children with special needs know how easy it is to push aside our personal lives - for our work to consume us.

## The Backyard Garden

*Today my son, Peter, has the task of picking a crop of cher-ries from the tree in our back yard. (I'll say "ugh" for him as he thinks about doing that in the hot sun). These beautiful little red creations serve our family in many ways and I'm anxious to pitch into caring for them. The strawberries have come and gone, much to my disappointment, the tomatoes are coming on like crazy and our little garden patch is overflowing with things in-cluding great-looking raspberries. My goodness, God is breaking out all over the place today, the corn here in Indiana is as high as an elephant's eye and I know God sees it and that it is good.*

*I think these little metaphors of cherries, corn and raspberries are outward signs of the inward creating and re-creating powers of God to make each of us fruitful and productive persons in all the places and professions where God finds us. It was human be-ings just like us who are called "....the planting of the Lord." I like to think this morning that whoever and wherever we are we have been planted there for a purpose. To accomplish that purpose God feeds and waters us in our spirits, gives us soil in which to grow, and rejoices when we bear fruit. What did we expect when we be-came clinicians or scientists or teachers or nurses or appliers of the knowledge we've gained through education and experience? Was it money? Prestige? Was it to be recognized and acclaimed by our peers? I think, on this third day of Creation, it is time for me in my own life to examine this.*

THERE'S A TON OF CHERRIES THIS YEAR AND IF YOU WERE CLOSE BY I'D INvite you to come and gather some for yourself. I go back to the reason God created the cherry tree I've sent Peter out to labor over. I don't think the purpose was to bear apples. Wordsworth wrote, "A primrose by a river's brim; A yellow primrose was to him, and it was nothing more." ("Peter Bell", Part 1, st. xxi). I think that is a hard lesson. When a primrose is only a primrose, when a patient is only a patient, when our profession is only to enhance our "success," when our family gets the dregs of our energy and attention, we are only a primrose and not an instrument by which God lives out his will of hope and healing for the world being created.

## Lessons in a Garden

I HAVE BEEN INSPIRED ALL MY ADULT LIFE BY THE EXAMPLE OF GREGOR MENDEL, an Austrian monk who, in his little monastery garden at Brunn, discovered many of the principles of plant genetics. His experiments weren't with oak trees, fields of wheat or giant forests, but with the lowly garden pea. He once summed up his whole purpose as a monk as one which was to show the glories of God in a garden. Likewise, In Voltaire's "Candide", the main character, Pangloss sums up the whole meaning of his life by saying at the end, "We must cultivate our garden."

Yes, of course, we must cultivate our professional skills, we hone our expertise, we sharpen our techniques and improve the technology to bring new life and healing to our patients or students. But now, on this third day of Creation, with all God's beauty and bounty, all this rich abundance of flora and fauna, I ask myself, what am I doing in this Garden? The question is not about work; I know what my work is. The question is about the person I am in the midst of everything around me, how my vocation and home life fit into a coherent whole that brings such joy and satisfaction, when I give it the attention it deserves.

We are called, I believe, in our relationships with family and friends to cultivate our gardens of inward serenity, strength of character, the capacity to love and forgive, to do our best and see the best in others - to be "plantings of the Lord." In Abraham Lincoln's words, to show others and ourselves, "….the better angels of our nature." I have always loved that expression from Lincoln's First Inaugural address.

## No Energy left for Family

YES, OF COURSE, I STRUGGLE WITH THIS AS EVERYONE DOES. I CAN RELATE so strongly with the mother who told her young children in no uncertain terms she was tired and busy and in no mood for their foolishness. They had errands to run and she just wanted to get them done as quickly as possible because she was so tired. She put the children in the car on the way to the dreaded grocery store, and stopped for gas. The mother spoke cheerily to the gas station attendant,

"Fill it up, please". From the backseat, one of the youngsters looked at his mother, confused and said, "But, Mama, you weren't tired with that man." My heart aches as I write this because I probably did and said things like that more times to my own children than I'll ever remember. I know my boys learned about moods fairly early, and they knew that sometimes their mother was in a grouchy or down mood when she had had a hard day at work. When Peter was about three, he knew lots of adjectives for emotions but wasn't sure of their exact meaning. Once, after getting home from a stressful day at work, I was impatient with him. His little face crumpled and he said, "Well, Mommy, you don't have to be so jealous with me." He had heard the word "jealous" but didn't really understand its exact meaning. His innocent three-year old brain did know that it was the description of a negative emotion, and he sensed my negativity very deeply, searching his vocabulary for something to describe it.

## Cultivating our Personal Gardens

I HAVE HAD DISCUSSIONS WITH SOME OF MY COLLEAGUES ABOUT THIS TENSION between commitment to work and commitment to our family and personal relationships. There have been times when I felt guilty that, because of pressing deadlines, I had spent several consecutive evenings writing reports or typing letters to insurance companies trying to justify authorization of speech services for a child. Sometimes I would resolve that, for that evening, I would not work, I would spend time with Clay and my boys, probably watching a basketball game (this is Indiana, after all) and eating popcorn. As the evening progressed, I would begin to feel anxious knowing I wasn't getting work done that was important to some child's future. If the parents of my patient, Sarah, didn't get my letter in time to submit it to the Hearing Officer, they might lose in their due process hearing and Sarah would be placed in an inappropriate classroom for the year. So there I sat, neither getting the paperwork done, nor really enjoying the time with my family. I find this to be one of my greatest struggles in this profession: Can we leave the office and "turn off" the burdens, the responsibilities of our work in order to be there wholly for our families, our friends, ourselves? Can I find in me a whole person, a whole clinician who is not consumed by my work?

I look back with shame at times when I have conducted seven or eight hour-long therapy sessions in a single day, mustering patience, good humor and self-control when interacting with these difficult children and their parents, yet when my own children came home, I was grumpy, or brushed them off, saying I needed to make an important phone call before I could talk to them about their day. Or, I snapped at Clay when he came home, also from a stressful day at work. At these moments, I resent my work – or should I say, I resent what I let my work do to me – choosing others over the ones I love and cherish most deeply – my own family.

As I struggle with the balance between family and work and all the obligations of my life, I take some small comfort in knowing that someone as centered and seemingly in control as Anne Morrow Lindbergh was tormented by how to achieve this very same balance in her life. She writes in *Gift from the Sea* that, "I want to have my family, to carry out my obligations to them." But she goes on to say that first and foremost, and as an end to these other desires, she wanted to be at peace with herself. Lindberg writes of yearning to live "in grace" as often as possible but does not use that term in its strictly theological sense. By grace, she explained, she meant "....an inner harmony, essentially spiritual, which can be translated into outward harmony. But, the life I have chosen entrains a whole caravan of complications....a circus act. This is not the life of simplicity but the life of multiplicity that leads not to unification but to fragmentation. It does not bring grace; it destroys the soul. I am seeking perhaps what Socrates asked for in the prayer from the *Phaedrus* when he said, 'May the outward and inward person be at one.' " Lindbergh's quest is similar to the concept Carl Rogers referred to as congruence; that the three aspects of who we are - our essence, our self-perception and the behavior we show to others - be in alignment. Rogers wrote that achieving congruence meant living "from the inside out." I like that expression.

## The Tug-of-War

IN THE MIDST OF WANTING TO LIVE FROM THE INSIDE OUT, HOW DO WE combat the tug-of-war between the family and friends outside of work whom we deeply cherish and the strain and stress of responsibility for our patients? How do we find the point where, "The outward and inward person are at one?" I have to confess this balance has been precarious for me. On the one hand, I want to live authentically, so that my life is unified. I don't want a double standard between how I treat people or think of myself at home and with friends versus how I behave or treat people in my work. Like Lindberg, I am striving for "the outward and inward person", (or should I say, the private and the professional person?) "to be at one."

But, wait. I do want some separation between those two elements of my life! My husband and children should not be constantly subjected to conversation over the dinner table about my frustration with the inequities of how Birth-to-Three services are administered in our state. My friends shouldn't have to listen to my irritation over the mountains of paperwork required just to get a child the speech therapy she's entitled to in the first place. When I think of my family, especially, they should get all of me - mentally, emotionally, attentionally - when I am home, not just the pieces of me that remain after the rest have been spent on my patients and their families. My own family and friends deserve the best of me, not just the left-overs.

To stand in the tragic gap, in this instance, means that I am willing to hold the tensions between those two worlds of my life, accepting that there will never be complete harmony between them, yet not allowing myself to be defeated by the challenges that will inevitably exist each time I must make a choice between family commitments and work commitments. When I am able to hold those tensions, I find I can be creative and energetic. I can be attentive and spirited with my patients, nurturing and supportive with my family, making some mistakes along the way and never accomplishing perfection. Never. Part of holding that tension is that I know I do not have to do it alone. God is beside me, and so are the trusted colleagues who each make a unique contribution to the care of our little patients. I could not do my work without these colleagues, as each of us holds up our small edge of the parachute that allows special-needs children and their families to stay airborne and sometimes even to soar. "Never doubt that a small group of committed citizens can change the world," wrote Margaret Mead. "It's the only thing that ever has."

## Transition Rituals for Clinicians and Children

ONE OF THE WAYS I HAVE FOUND TO BE MORE FULLY PRESENT BOTH IN MY professional and personal live is to practice some transition habits when I go from home life to work life, and vice versa. Just as our students needs time to close their Math books, clear their minds of long division before opening their literature book, so I need such transitions. I have talked to some clinicians who have developed effective rituals for this transition. I learned of some transition rituals from Kenny, a speech-language pathologist whom I met at an ASHA meeting in Chicago when we both attended a group called FOCUS or Forum On the Clinical Use of Spirituality (did you even know this group existed? I didn't until that time.) Kenny teaches a classroom for children with language-impairment in a challenging neighborhood school in Los Angeles and his most important part of the day is the transition between his home and the school where he works. He shared how he listened each morning to a recording on his iPod during his bus ride to work. The recordings were chants and calming music from the traditions of Eastern religions, particularly Buddhism. It was fascinating to hear him share his techniques for working with students, especially the Buddhist tradition of looking for the space between breaths. As Kenny spoke in our group, I was amazed at his calm demeanor, especially as he described a classroom where two or three children are in foster care and have a limited sense of bonding or trust with any adult; one of his students is a Jehovah Witness and is not allowed to refer to any of his non-Witness classmates as "friends." Yet, Kenny was deeply committed to ensuring that every day, each of his students knew he cared about them. Kenny is one example of the many devoted, caring clinicians whom I admire in this profession.

He has established a structure in his classroom of an appreciation circle that begins each morning and sets the tone for the day. His personal transitions on the way to work inspired the transitions he established for his students, many of whom came from disorder or even violence in the home. His morning appreciation circle transitioned them to a place of learning, energy, and above all, trust. As Kenny spoke, I was reminded of the poem, "The Other Side of the Door" by Jeff Moss. It is reprinted in *Teaching With Fire – Poems that sustain the courage to*

*Teach* (S. Intrator & Scribner, Editors.) The teacher, Lamson T. Lam, who submitted the poem to that volume writes that he has posted it outside the classroom door in every school in which he's taught, including under-resourced and challenging schools in the Bronx. It is an assurance to the children about the magic of learning, the threshold they cross to a place of trust and infinite possibilities when they open the door and enter their classroom. What a powerful message to receive. Kenny's practices have prompted me to suggest some other transitions that may help us be more fully present with our family and friends.

## The "Who Is There?" Transition

Thich Nhat Hanh, a Buddhist sage, advises all of us to take a deep breath before answering the telephone, using a practice he calls, "Who Is Here Today?" Irwin Kula, in *Yearnings,*, extends this suggestion and applies it to the transition period between work and home life. After a long day at the office, before opening the door to his home, Kula says he pauses, takes a deep breath and asks himself, "Irwin, are you home?" I use this often, after I shut the door to my home office and come downstairs to greet my children from school or my husband as he comes into the house in the evening. I ask myself, "Amy, are you home? Are you really home?"

## Physical Activity

Physical exercise re-focuses our attention, especially if, as in my case, you're not very athletic. It takes all my concentration to finish on the weight machine in the gym, or better yet, play a set of tennis with a friend. The swirling thoughts that want to crowd my mind about a patient's problem or that article that needs review find no room in a mind concentrating so hard on returning a backhand down-the-line shot. Exercise has additional physiological benefits in the body's release of mood-elevating neurotransmitters. We feel happier after we are physically active! It is a way to temporarily leave work behind us, whether done alone as a transition between work and home, or done with an exercise partner.

## Lay your Burdens Down in Writing

Have you ever tried writing down your unresolved work worries or tasks at the end of the work day, keeping them safe but cloistered, so they do not contaminate your home life? Similarly, when home and family concerns weigh upon me as I work, I try to write those down early in the morning and put them in a box at home. A wise psychotherapist here in Indianapolis, Dr. Dorothy Wittenberg, has taught me about the liberating act of writing down our troubles. We give ourselves permission to worry about them and to deal with them, but not right now. Writing down our concerns is an assurance that we will give these issues the attention they deserve, when the time is right. It also helps us externalize an issue – to make it something outside ourselves that we can deal with, rather than harboring it internally where it may fester and vex us.

# Music Soothes The Soul

Music is an important transition tool for me, especially because I have a home office and my boys may be coming in the door just as my last patient is leaving for the day. My actual transition time might be nil, but I can create a transition "mood" by putting on music that evokes a particular feeling or sense of home and family. While I'm asking my boys about their day, preparing dinner, this music is a reminder that I've shifted from work gear to family gear. Tastes in music are so personal, I know I can't prescribe a certain genre or artist that everyone would enjoy. And that's the beauty of music and the way it appeals to different people. Some listeners find great peace in classical music, my oldest son studies while listening to stirring opera arias (these would probably just make me feel nervous at the end of the day, but they are perfect for him.) Find the music that is most helpful to you as you transition from work life to home life. When the music involves up-beat vocals, I sometimes make myself sing along. If I sing the songs aloud, I just may begin feeling what I am singing. Music changes behavior and behavior changes mood. Period.

Though I may sometimes be drawn to energetic pop music, at other times I crave the sound of calming folksingers. I think their wistful voices slow the heart rate, make us lean in and give us pause. Carrie Newcomer, a Bloomington, Indiana-based singer is my favorite. Her words often seem to be written just for me, and her melodies, and the strength of her deep voice is moving every time I hear it. In a twist of synchronicity her husband, Robert Meitus, is the son of Irv Meitus, a speech pathology mentor of mine who, with his wife, took me under his wing when I started my graduate program at Purdue. Irv died several years ago and Robert and I only discovered this connection recently, but it made Carrie's music all the more meaningful. And, Irv would have loved a daughter-in-law who could compose and sing as Carrie can. One of my favorites, from her *The Gathering of Spirits* album, is her song, "I'll Go Too" about her father being at her side during important times of her life. Given the relationship I have with my father, this song evokes deep feelings in me about my dad. Of course songs have different personal meanings for each listener, but this one speaks to me of the gift we can offer of just being beside other people as they go through some of life's tough moments.

> *When I was learning how to swim,*
> *I'd look down at the water and back at him*
> *He'd say, "Take my hand, we'll both jump in*
> *I'll go, too.*
> *I'll go too, I'll go too"*
> *That's what he'd say and what he'd do.*
> *"Don't go alone I'll walk with you*
> *I'll go too."*

I have a collection of Scottish and other Celtic music, both the vocals and the instrumentals seem to resonate with my heritage. Is that possible? If you haven't heard

Connie Dover's, *The Border of Heaven* CD, subtitled *Celtic Music on the American Frontier*, it's a real gem. My other favorites are the CD's by Alex Beaton, including the songs, "Shoals of Herring," "My Cavan Girl," "These Are my Mountains" and his whole CD *Songs of Praise, Pipes of Peace* that includes one of my dad's favorite hymns, "Children of the Heavenly Father."

## Expressing our Creative Energy

Pablo Picasso said, "Art washes away from the soul the dust of everyday life." I've described listening to music, but like many of you, I also play an instrument, both as a form of relaxation and as a way to make the transition to a different state of mind. When I was a child, my mother told me she could tell what mood I was in by how I played the piano. I know this is still true today, because at any given time, I am drawn toward playing a particular piece on the piano that reveals the mood I'm in. I can hear the same echoing of mood when I hear my boys play the piano or guitar. One doesn't have to be a professional artist to draw deep satisfaction from creative endeavors. Meister Eckhart wrote, "An artist isn't a special kind of person; each person is a special kind of artist." Engaging in a creative art form is immensely satisfying, transports us away from the stresses of our work and taps into a part of us that wants to find expression. The theme of this book is Re-Creation, after all, and the creative process rejuvenates us, sometimes subtly, sometimes so powerfully we feel re-born. Perhaps you take a dance class, play a musical instrument, paint, take photographs, sculpt, knit, or, as my husband does, create artwork in the form of a delightful garden, a masterpiece of colorful flowers, greenery, bird sanctuaries and, yes cherry trees. In Clay's case, what "washes away the dust of everyday life" from his soul is the creation and sustaining of a garden.

## Eden

> I look out from this east window at the trees of Indianapolis and I think I might be looking at what Eden looked like when it had all been put together in the Beginning. Earth, vegetation, plants, seeds, trees, fruit, everything needed to sustain life for people and animals. But what really awes me as I look out at all this is that it's only the third day, there's so much more on the way! That awe is grounded in the power of change built into this whole work of creation beginning with the heavens and the earth and extending even to me and my ability to bring about change in my own life. This is the genius quality of something created by God's hand, the quality or power of replicating itself.

THIS THIRD DAY OF THE WEEK, WHEN VEGETATION AND FLORA WERE created, I think of a story of the Reverend John Chapman, a New England minister who emigrated westward during colonial days into this wilderness that was Ohio, Kentucky and Indiana in those days. He spent much of his time planting apple trees and of course became known as Johnny Appleseed. It is said that when John Chapman died he was taken up to heaven and shown the beauties of that celestial way of life. As he looked out all across that wide expanse of what must have been a cosmic Garden of Eden he said, "Why, this isn't heaven, this is the Ohio wilderness!" I think we who have inherited this Creation, this earth, moon, sun, stars and all of nature can't help but feel that our real heaven is the beauty of what we see out of our own windows. We taught our children the "Johnny Appleseed" grace when they were little and sometimes that's the prayer we still use before a meal: "….And so I thank the Lord, for giving me the things I need, the sun and the rain and the apple seed."

## Re-cultivating Our Gardens - Synchronicity

JUST AS JOHN CHAPMAN PLANTED THE SEEDS THAT WOULD GROW INTO FRUIT-bearing trees, so I believe there is the opportunity, each new day, to plant seeds and cultivate the gardens of our relationships with our friends, families, our spouses, our children. We can and should do that intentionally, of course, but sometimes the most satisfying shared moments come when we unexpectedly, without careful planning, seize the moment and do something spontaneous and unexpected with those we love. The poet Robert Frost goes so far as to even hope, "May much stay out of our stated plan." I had an experience once that was so far out of anyone's stated plan, it just couldn't have been anything but synchronicity, as Jung identified it. I had kept two journals during our year in Brussels. One was a professional journal, describing my experiences consulting with 3-M, traveling to snowy Stockholm in December where I saw multi-channel cochlear implant patients for the first time – patients who could understand speech with their implant! In the U.S., we only had access to single-channel implants at that time, and those patients could rarely understand speech with their device. But these European patients – unbelievable! I tried to describe this in my journal back then but did so inadequately. I should have stuck with the highly-technical description of a cochlear implant that a colleague uses, "It's a damn miracle!"

The other journal I kept was a personal, family journal, about our move to Brussels, our early months of marriage, and then, of finding out I was expecting our son, Campbell and the joy of experiencing pregnancy for the first time. After arriving home in Indianapolis after a year in Brussels, our luggage arrived and had been broken into during transit. Many things were missing from one suitcase including my personal, family journal. I was devastated. Who would steal a personal journal, I wondered in anger and sadness. The written notes of such special moments, including the first time I felt Campbell move inside me, were gone. After feeling sorry for myself, I moved on and sort of forgot about the stolen journal. A few weeks later, Herb, the jeweler who had sold Clay and me our wedding rings called. "Amy, I just got the oddest thing in the mail," Herb said. "It looks like some kind of a diary, and there is a note inside it for you." After racing to his shop and seeing the lost journal, I burst into tears. But how had it ended up back in Indianapolis, and why was it mailed to Herb? The letter inside explained all that. A woman wrote she had noticed the journal lying next to a trash can in the Philadelphia airport (we hadn't even flown through Philadelphia on our way home) and had picked it up, realizing it couldn't possibly be trash. The only identification in it, though, was the receipt I had saved when I bought Clay's wedding ring from Herb. It was an invoice with Herb's mailing address at the top, so she had taken a chance to mail it to Herb, hoping he would know how to contact us.

When Campbell was younger, he loved to look through the journal and read about what I was experiencing as he grew inside me and what life in Brussels was like. That journal is the link between members of our family, obviously unimportant to the person who broke into my luggage and discarded it. But, how grateful I will always be for the kindness of a complete stranger who took the time to return the journal to me, in a rather circuitous route, so that the link it represents in our family would not be broken.

## Grandmother's Bread

ANOTHER LINK IN OUR FAMILY IS BAKING AND COOKING, AND PASSING recipes down from generation to generation. I used to watch my Grandmother McConkey work new dough for morning baking. She would roll and pound, push and pull, shape and cut. The smell of her kitchen, actually the smell of her whole house during baking time, was a delight that is as fresh for me today as it was when I was a child, fascinated by her art and seduced by the smells. I watched the change of flour and water to a yeasty dough, and then to a loaf of steaming hot bread. Change, emergence, transformation is what Creation is about, something becoming something different, a person becoming a new person. That's the message of Genesis to me, beginning, changing, becoming. Jesus spoke of the new wine of the Spirit, old wine losing its flavor, new wine being tangy and flavorful. In that parable alone we see Creation, planted, gathered, yielding, bearing, appearing. Just as with Grandma's bread, don't we actually smell Creation, the earth after a rain, grass after mowing, cinnamon apples cooking, the dark humidity of woodland?

# An Unexpected Twist –
## How our Families benefit From Our Work

*In my efforts to practice my faith and to balance everything in my life I sometimes feel I'm down match point. God is always serving me aces I think I can't handle, especially in the form of fearing I have neglected my own family in favor of my patients. But, I have also seen the benefit my three sons have received from witnessing their mother's vocation. This process, though, is revealed in its own time. As St. Vincent de Paul wrote, "Nature demands that trees be deeply rooted before they can bear fruit and this is a gradual process."*

I KNOW THIS IS TRUE FOR MANY OF YOU, MY COLLEAGUES WHO HAVE SPOKEN about your children's or partner's increased sense of empathy because they have watched your work or met your clients. Several years ago, one of my sons who was about seven, went to a school carnival and came home to proudly show me the prizes he had picked out from his arcade winnings. "Look, Mom," he told me. "Here's a little bell and a clacker-thing you can use with your patients!" My middle son, Luke, usually the first one home from school and therefore most likely to see my patients, will sometimes offer just the thing a parent needs to hear, completely unprompted by me. "Hi, Justin," he'll say, and then have a little conversation with my patient. Luke will often comment to the child's parent, "Wow, his speech is really getting better, isn't it?" and I am grateful for the sensitivity and tenderness he has shown at just the right moment.

My colleague, Adeline, tells of a family tradition her Irish father instilled in her and that she passed along to her own children. Her father taught Adeline to imagine she wore an invisible sign around her neck that said, "I'm lovable, I'm capable and I'm *learning* to be responsible." This was a reminder to a child both of her inherent worth and also that we are all "in process" - none of us has achieved perfection. Adeline said that more than once, her young children came home dejected after a hard day at school and said, "Mom, I think I need a new invisible sign." So, they shared in the process of "removing" the tattered one and exchanging it, and her child's self-esteem, with a fresh replacement. Adeline has gone on to share this technique with the families of her pediatric patients with hearing loss. In this, as in many other cases, lessons of value crossed the boundaries between home and work and enhanced lives in both places.

*I wonder, "Why aren't there any cherries among all the fruits listed in the Bible?" Was it because God knew somehow beforehand I would claim that to get Peter up and at his task? Or that the heavenly Father knew what would happen to the health of his yet-to-be-created people when they discovered those things could be made into pies? I was having fun with God there, I think he likes to have fun, he invented it. But in and through everything of this created earth there is the blessed stamp of God's approval, "And God saw that it was good." Especially cherry pie.*

*I close my journal with, "And there was morning and there was evening, the third day."*

# Resources for Re-creation of Personal Relationships and Family Life

## Individual Resources

1. Think about which of the transition techniques mentioned in the chapter might be useful to you. Practice the "Who Is Here?" transition as a beginning point.

2. Books have been written about the power of being in the outdoors, taking a walk and watching and listening for the sounds of the natural world. Making a ritual of walking with a friend or your spouse can feel like a cleansing of the residue of work and a taking in of the other treasures in our life. If I can't find serenity in my own world, I often get going into God's world! When I can't go outside, I find that even playing a DVD of nature sounds is soothing.

3. Music changes our mood and our mood changes our behavior. Think of the music that puts you in the "I'm away from work" mode, whether it's upbeat Oldies, Classical, Opera or your own personal choices.

4. Spend time with friends who don't share your work. How liberating it is to have an evening out, or invite friends to our home who share common interests but don't work with us and don't know enough to delve into our job problems. It gives us a respite from the issues at work that trouble us.

## Group Resources

1. What obstacles do you face transitioning from home to work and back home? Share thoughts on what you have found that makes the transition smoother. Exercise? What about writing down your worries? Are you willing to experiment with the "Who Is Here?" technique.

2. We spoke of the power of music, yet it is only one of many creative outlets that renew us. Do you relax after work by listening to music, or do you play an instrument or sing, paint, use a pottery wheel, sketch or dance?

3. We deeply value our families and friendships, yet they sometimes seem to take second place. Did these words from earlier in this chapter resonate with you: My own family and friends should get all of me when I am home, not just the pieces of me that remain after the rest have been spent on my work. They deserve the best of me, not just the left-overs. How can we safeguard our family and friends from just getting the "left-overs" of who we are?

4. Boundaries are important for the issues we have discussed. What pressures at work strain or even cross the boundaries you want to have between your professional and work lives? Talk about strategies for securing those boundaries.

5. The importance of a rich and fulfilling life that includes our work but is not limited to it is the essence of this chapter. Talk about the resources for finding that fulfillment outside your job that make you energized to go to work on Monday mornings. Don't forget about what your own back yard holds. On a warm rainy day, try sitting in your garden (maybe even making a mud pie.)

# THE FOURTH DAY

# RE-CREATION WITHIN CONFLICT

*And God said, "Let them be for signs and for seasons and for days and years…" (Gen. 1:14)*

*To everything there is a season…….(Eccles. 3:1)*

*Have you learned lessons only from those who*
*admired you and were tender with you and stood*
*aside for you? Have you not learned great lessons*
*from those who braced themselves against you and*
*disputed the passage with you?*
*-Walt Whitman*

SITTING ON MY PATIO THIS EARLY MORNING AS I OFTEN DO WHEN WEATHER permits, I watch two blue jays scolding each other as they swirl around and above the big fountain. They fly at each other, collide high above the lawn, dart and make bird noises that sound like warnings, actually push and shove each other in endless combat. One of them wants his own space on one of the tiers of the fountain and doesn't seem willing to share his spot under any circumstances. I don't really know if they're playing games or establishing territory or celebrating the morning. It wouldn't surprise me at all if they are actually having an argument. If they are, then I shall welcome them to my world which is, to my dismay and sorrow, a world of conflict and endless animosity. There isn't anything new about this kind of world. I guess it's been that kind of world from the beginning.

*A look at my scripture reading this fourth morning of re-creation, a reading of the creation of times and seasons and I can't but feel a sadness on behalf of God who "made everything good in its time." Even within my small world of family, friends and colleagues there is enormous pain arising from conflict. I have dear friends who are wasting away emotionally and economically, in bitter and pro-longed divorce. There are families in the school environment of our boys who seem never to break out of the cycle of shouting, accusing, threatening and humiliating each other. Everyday we see public fig-ures in government, private enterprise, religion, academia and the arts confronting each other with threats and counter threats. No wonder Mercutio, weary with fighting between the houses of the Montagues and the Capulets, cried out in desperation, "A plague on both your houses!"*

## Ever-Present Conflict

WHEN I CONSIDER MY LIFE, I WONDER HOW MUCH OF IT I SPEND IN CON-flict. I suspect it is more than I know. Much of that is mental of course, inward struggle against real or imagined adversaries -honestly, I don't usually begin the day with a sword fight in the street (although I may be locked in battle with the nasty pile of laundry accumulating in my basement.) What I mean is that I rarely awake without the awareness of some past, present or future conflict between myself and others, sometimes even with members of my own family, conflict between ideas, views, strategies and intentions. Most of these are minor run-of-the-mill kinds of things, easily resolved, quickly forgotten, successfully dealt with. Something simple will do, a word of explanation or clarification, a gesture of reconciliation, an apology, giving way. But not always. Sometimes these conflicts are serious, at least they seem so. They have lasting implications, to avoid them is to compound them. I wonder if I, like many, find some sort of self-serving satisfaction in not making peace with someone who has wronged me. In *Gilead*, Marilynne Robinson writes, "I have always liked the phrase 'nursing a grudge' because many people are tender of their resentments, as of the things nearest their hearts" (p. 117). We may spend a lot of energy protecting and nursing our grudges.

## *Conflict, Stubbornness and Pride*

THE THEME I WRITE ABOUT TODAY is that of re-creating ourselves after conflict. No, I think it is more accurate to say, within conflict, because I'm not sure any of us, including me, is ever completely free of conflict in our professional and personal lives. Of course, some conflict is a result of our upholding a principle so deeply felt that we would betray ourselves if we did not defend it. But, what about the frequent, petty conflict focused on issues that aren't worth fighting about. Why does pride play such an important, but sometimes dangerous, role in human relationships? When we mix pride with stubbornness we create a lethal concoction of trouble. In Carl Sandburg's poem, "Primer Lesson," he warns:

> Look out how you use proud words.
> When you let proud words go, it is not easy to call
> them back.
> They wear long boots, hard boots; they walk off
> proud; they
> can't hear you calling –
> Look out how you use proud words.
> 　　　-Carl Sandburg

The rising and falling of conflicts due to stubbornness or resentment or "proud words that wear hard boots" seems to have the same cycles as the seasons of the year. The seasons represent a rhythm, a symbol of our relationships as they oscillate between harmony and disharmony. There is a spring to our relationships where "all's right with the world." A summer of parched friendship neglect can be a warning of sad things coming. The fall months often mean a new intensity of work, commitments and involvements and the possibility of a new outbreak of disagreements or a resurrection of old ones. A "winter of our discontent" can make the November and December holidays more of a burden than a moveable feast.

# Conflict, Faith and the Goal

S o, as I consider the meaning of this fourth day of Creation I think my religious faith is knocking at my door wanting in. I have read that the early days of the Christian community, one that has its roots in the faith and beliefs of Jewish life surrounding Jesus, that this community was one of mind-boggling conflict. The disciples disagreed with Jesus, they disagreed among themselves, Jesus disagreed with the religious and political leaders around him and it's a wonder to me that anything at all was accomplished during those days. That so much was done can be traced I think to the fact that most of these disagreers (I think I just made up a new word), were of the same mind as to the goal. That goal was how best to witness to the saving acts of God in the world.

Well, my goodness, doesn't this tell us that so many of our conflicts are not about the goal but about how to reach the goal? In a football game the decision is, shall we kick it, pass it, run it or fake it? Whatever the disagreement about how it will be done eventually all understand and cooperate in putting the ball across the goal line. I think we take sides too easily, we forget there is often a middle ground, a huddle wherein we observe the rules of teamwork, exercise patience, show professionalism, give a little, back off, "show a little kindness." "He is our peace," wrote Paul in Ephesians 2:14, "who has made us one and has broken down the dividing wall of hostility....thereby bringing the hostility to an end."

But I'll tell you something, there are times for all of us when that goal line can seem awfully far away and our chances of getting there slimmer and slimmer. I'm not the first person to find that the playing field of life isn't always even. Life is lived vertically as well as horizontally. We walk forward and backward but we walk uphill and downhill as well. We walk against inertia and discouragement, against pride and stubbornness and that can be a long and hard walk. I have found that a major contributor to conflict for me is looking at things too narrowly, with a focus on the short-term, without seeing the longer-term, wider viewpoint.

What lessons I have learned from Christopher Monger's book and the movie of the same title *The Englishman Who Went Up a Hill but Came Down a Mountain*. Based upon real events, this story tells how a small Welsh town - whose citizens are frequently at odds with one another - faces a communal crisis. The only thing in which all its citizens take pride is the fact the village lies on the slope of the first mountain one encounters when entering Wales from England. This distinction is threatened when a new land survey downgrades the prized mountain to a mere hill, prompting the townspeople to construct a plan that will transform their hill into a mountain again. What I see in this story of a Welsh village is first, that we so often manufacture our own mountains! But I also see how, in the face of a perceived obstacle, a community bands together for a shared purpose, replacing dissention and conflict with cooperation and, ultimately, unexpected sacrifice.

Life is a journey upward in learning, growing, being equipped for what we must do and what we must be. Often it is the mountains scaled rather than the even path walked that turn out to be the supreme moments of our lives. To scale a height is to be able to see the view from the top. As a teenage boy from western Kansas, my father served in the Marine Corps during the second World War and observed the famous raising of the flag on Suribachi. He says in his book, *Fickle Gods of Iwo Jima*, that while on the ground in heavy fighting, he saw only the immediate, the horrific, the moment-by-moment reality of trying to stay alive. But, once on top of that mountain he and the others "could see all that could not be seen from below, the wide, wide sea, other islands, the entire landscape of Iwo Jima. It was a moment of exhilaration to see things from a mountaintop," even in the midst of the horrendous conflict going on below.

## Creation of the Seasons

*My reading from Genesis calls to mind Franz Joseph Haydn's great oratorio, "The Creation." In music only a Haydn could create, this great Austrian composer put into musical form the power and splendor of the four seasons. In this oratorio he creates sounds from the orchestra that parallel the sounds of birds in spring, rain in summer, crisp mornings in the fall and the hard feel of winter cold. I have listened to "The Creation" with the text of the words in front of me and have actually felt the sensation of these seasons. Haydn also wrote the oratorio "The Seasons" in which he recreated other sounds and feels of the changing year. In our church on Sunday morning we sometimes sing the great hymn, "The Spacious Firmament on High", the tune from Hayden's, "The Creation." When I sing it I sometimes get so caught up in the majesty of this music:*

> *"Soon as the evening shades prevail, the moon
> takes up the wondrous tale,
> And nightly, to the listening earth, repeats the
> story of her birth.
> While all the stars that round her burn, and all the
> planets in their turn,
> Confirm the tidings as they roll, and spread the
> truth from pole to pole."*

Ah, yes, ".....THE MOON TAKES UP THE WONDROUS TALE...." THIS FOURTH day of Creation is the day the sun and the moon came into existence in the Genesis account. We know the sun for what it is. It gives light, warmth, healing, promise of a new day, life itself. "The lesser light" as the moon is called in the creation story is for moonlight, sleep, romance, poetry, imagination, star gazing, and contemplation that we see a face there. Yet the moon, for all its use, or misuse, as a symbol of love and poetic inspiration, is an instrument of majestic power and cosmic intention. The great tides and surges of the oceans are the handiwork of the moon. The pull of that heavenly body is what fishermen fish by, sailors sail by and swimmers swim by. So steadfast, dependable and faithful is the moon that high, low and neap tides can be predicted as far into the future as infinity. Dave Sindrey shared that he has always viewed the moon as a symbol of comfort and constancy, because no matter where we stand on the planet earth, we all see exactly the same side of the moon. The moon has a certain fascination for most children. Dave, for example, read stories to his children about the moon. Chris Barton composed a song, "Mama, Can you Turn on the Moon?" after her son posed that very question to her. My father taught my children a little good night prayer "I see the moon; the moon sees me. God bless the moon, and God bless me."

It has always fascinated me that in the Hebrew language the word for a new moon also describes the concept of renewal (Job 26:9; Ps. 81:3). In God's creative process both the sun and the moon, light and darkness, morning and evening, are symbols of new life from old. My Grandma Ocie had the perfect understanding of this with her comment, "Morning is for showing us what God has done during the night."

Well, I need to come back down to earth here this morning and see what God has done during the night on this fourth day of creation. This isn't hard for me to do at all, since I live in the Midwest where we have four distinct seasons, about as distinct as four seasons can be. I have friends in places in the United States and in the world where there is only one season that is pretty much the same year round. And, I spent seven of my growing-up years in equatorial Panama where there were, in fact two seasons – rainy season and dry season, although the temperature and humidity were constants, and it was only the rainfall that differentiated the two seasons. Living back in the States now, I am glad to have the four seasons again. I love the crisp fall air just as I love the summer sunshine and a beautiful snowfall comes about as close to something direct from God as anything I know.

## *Promises of the Seasons*

> *The seasons, like so much else in this wonderful world God has created and is creating now, have built in promises to them. Just from the Book of Genesis itself God makes sure we understand the dependability of the way things are put together. "As long as the earth endures, seedtime and harvest, cold and heat, summer and winter, day and night, shall not cease" (Gen. 8:22.)*

> *I need this dependability of things to help match my "Intend to" with my "It's accomplished." There always seems to be a gap between those in my life and I have to work hard not to let my inten-*

*tions exceed the time I have to reach those intentions. Today is Thursday in this cycle of days and I have to make a very special effort to sustain that "Keep a-goin'" of my Grandmother McConkey. This is especially true of the winter months and the tail end of the week days where I would sometimes just like to stay in bed, or go back to bed, and pull up the covers over my head or watch the snow fall and pretend I'm a moth in a cocoon. On Thursdays sometimes I have to fight off ennui.*

## Conflict with Patients and Their Families

HUMAN BEINGS WHO INTERACT ON A REGULAR BASIS WILL INEVITABLY experience some degree of conflict. Any of you will testify to conflict in our profession. We know this risk of conflict is particularly acute in situations where emotions run high, where there is depth of feeling, especially of grief or pain. Clinicians know the emotional layer, often very deep and wide, that accompanies our relationship with children with special needs and their parents. And that layer can create an atmosphere of tension, misunderstanding and, yes, conflict. My Canadian colleague, Carolyne Edwards has written about conflict with parents who at the surface level may be resistant to our ideas about the management of their children with special needs. Carolyne has taught me a lot about the fact that the resistance is often the surface form of a deeper emotion of fear or mistrust that a parent is feeling. Our initial response is sometimes to respond in kind, that is, to be stern with families who are being "uncooperative" or resistant to the suggestions we provide for their child. Though we try to remain objective, it is also hurtful when parents blame the messenger and become angry or hostile with us, who sadly, have had to break the news of a difficult diagnosis. Resistance from families evokes a defensive response in many of us, resulting in a cycle of unpleasant conversations and a feeling of defeat. I know that I cannot provide the full potential of my therapy skills unless a family and I are in synch regarding the program we have set for their child. That means that, when I do sense resistance, I cannot simply ignore it, hoping it goes away. Yet, dealing with resistant parents is not easy, and for some of us, it's the last thing we want to do.

In teaching workshops over the last decade, I have heard repeatedly that conflict with parents is one of the things that is discouraging to those working in our profession. A teacher of special-needs children told me, "I love working with the children and I know how much more progress they make when the parents and teacher are aligned. But, I am at the end of my rope in dealing with hostile parents who immediately blame me for any problem, without calling or discussing things civilly." This clinician was expressing a tragic gap: the gulf between the satisfying, team-based relationship with parents that she craved – and felt was possible – and the reality of conflict and finger-pointing that existed in her job.

## Not the What but the How

THERE ARE TIMES I NEED TO TALK TO FAMILIES HONESTLY ABOUT uncomfortable subjects such as their resistance to recommendations or their failure to follow a protocol that will lead to full-time hearing aid use by their child. But how I say the words in the midst of conflict is the critical thing that may determine my relationship with a family for years to come, creating either a bond of trust and respect between us or one of resentment. For many of us, our physical posture and speaking style sends an underlying message to families of either acceptance or criticism, and most of us did not take Counseling courses during our graduate school that would help us know about these subtle messages. But, we must take care to notice them and improve them. Above all, we must ensure that we are listening, really listening, to what parents tell us, and not just waiting for a break in their speech to start talking. A Native American proverb says, "Listen, or your tongue will keep you deaf." Some clinicians have to be particularly aware of their body posture when interacting with families, such as not speaking to parents from behind a desk with arms crossed in a posture of power. I have had a colleague who worked hard to maintain eye contact when speaking to parents about a child's progress or lack thereof, because she became aware of her tendency to look away when speaking to families. This gave the erroneous impression that she was not a caring person. For me, I have to watch my tone of voice, it can become preachy when I don't mean it to be. *"Behold how much wood is kindled by how small a fire, and the tongue is a fire" (James 3:6.)*

Two important sources help me prepare myself for uncomfortable conversations with parents: nature and prayer. It is not surprising that R.M. Rilke connects those two sources when he writes that when we go into nature, "Our breathing deepens and our hearts calm…….. When serenity is restored, new perspectives open to us and difficulty can begin to seem like an invitation to new growth. This is also the experience of prayer" (O'Donohue, p. 17.) After that preparation, I can more easily enter into dialogue with resistant parents. I try to use the techniques Carolyne Edwards has taught me about the underlying message I send, which is one of optimism, and the words I use, which should be non-defensive. I have learned to approach parents saying something like, "Mr. and Mrs. Jones, I wanted to talk to you today about Billy. I think I can help him – I really believe I have a system of techniques that would help him learn. But, I need your support at home and want to know if you feel you can be part of that system. It would involve your reinforcing the concepts we use at school, and reviewing his vocabulary sheets with him. I think this could be more effective than what we are doing now, and your help at home is so important to his success." This type of message conveys a hopefulness that all of us need to feel if we are to take on something that is challenging and also uses honest language that does not point a finger of blame. The Resources section at the end of this chapter provides additional suggestions for managing conflict with patients' families.

## The White Hat Approach to Conflict

I HAVE COME TO RECOGNIZE, TOO, THAT AT TIMES I AM THE ONE DOING THE resisting when families ask me to do things a certain way, or request a particular technique that is unfamiliar to me. It may disrupt my already unsteady apple-cart of plans and goals and objectives for that child. During such times, I try at least to consider the ideas of the parents, and to think back on the principles of *The Six Thinking Hats,* a little gem of a book shared with me by Dave Sindrey. When first confronting a conflict, author Edward DeBono suggests we put on only our "white thinking hat" - the hat that forces us to look solely at the facts and disallows the consideration of emotion (the red hat) or intuition (the green hat.) The latter two may be extremely important to decision-making, but those hats will be worn separately, when I am ready to consider my emotion and my intuition. I have found, only recently I might add, that if I allow myself to put on my white hat and focus strictly on facts, I may find that the parents have a very legitimate idea that is better than my own! But the rub is, I'll have to change what I had already planned and that is hard for me, and I suspect, for many of us. The Roman writer and statesman, Publius Syrus said, "It's a bad plan that can't be changed," and I have come to expect that most of my grand ideas will eventually require at least some change, and that's not half bad. It's just getting used to the idea that is difficult. And, just as my own children respect me more when I say, "You know, you're right, now that you've explained in that way, I have changed my mind and will compromise with you and let you go to the party," so families increase their respect when they realize their child's teacher is willing to change and adapt, out of respect for the families and in the presence of new information.

## Healing the Patient or Curing the Pathology?

I T IS ALSO THE CASE THAT PARENTS SOMETIMES BECOME RESISTANT TO OUR efforts when they sense that we are looking only at the disability of their child (in my case, "broken ears" or "broken speech") rather than at the child as a whole, or even more importantly, the family as a whole. Paul Brenner writes that because the body is viewed in Western medicine as being too complex for any one individual to understand fully, we've divided the body into parts. "Knowing about a part has replaced feeling about the whole. Time restraints also have contributed to the loss of a holistic outlook. As a result, both the [health care provider] and the patient have been diminished, and the art of healing the person has been lost to the science of curing the pathology" (p. 7.)

Yet the fact remains, often hard for those of us in helping professions to accept, that there are situations beyond our control. Situations where, in spite of our best efforts, our energy and our prayers, we cannot change a child, or his parents, or a certain social structure within a family, or an unyielding school district. In those moments, I say Reinhold Niebuhr's prayer, the prayer I probably have most often used over the twenty-plus years of my work: "God, grant me the serenity to accept the things I cannot change, the courage to change the things I can, and the wisdom to know the difference." This of course, is the guiding prayer of Alcoholics Anonymous.

## Conflicts with Colleagues

AS MUCH AS I LOVE OUR GARDEN WITH ALL ITS BEAUTY OF COLOR AND WILD-life, I have already described the conflict that persists within it. And I acknowledge, shamefully, that the conflict I see in my garden is also in me, and in the interactions I may have with colleagues. Here in the garden of my heart is where so much of the violence of the world takes place, in miniature. This violence is my capacity for anger, jealousy, lovelessness, contrariness, stubbornness, unforgiveness, all of it from A to Z. I am the weeds in my own garden. Here is where I rise or fall as a human being in my effort for "going on to perfection" as John Wesley described it. There is a seasonal rhythm to this I know. Often I experience the springtime of sudden spurts of spiritual enthusiasm in which instantaneously I want to become a model of virtue. Before I know it the world intrudes on that resolution and I find myself dropping back into a winter of personal dissatisfaction. This is why discipline is so important to me even though I practice it imperfectly. Disciplines of prayer and meditation, reading and public worship, are my stimuli to move from springtime to the fullness of summer.

## Conflict and the Seasons - The Channel between Voice and Presence

MOST OF US DON'T CHOOSE OUR COLLEAGUES, THE PEOPLE WITH WHOM WE spend the majority of our days – sometimes more hours per week than are spent with our own families. Think of the number of verbal interactions we might have in the course of a week with co-workers, and the potential consequences of those interactions. I try to remind myself of the words of the Gautama, Buddha, "Whatever words we utter should be chosen with care, for people will hear them and be influenced by them for good or ill." Being a Christian or a Jew or a spiritual person does not mean that conflict won't exist in one's life. As someone quipped re-framing a famous Bible verse, "Wherever two or more are gathered in His name, there is conflict."

Just as in each season nature deals differently with its bounty, so different situations of conflict in our workplaces require different responses. This is the gift I have observed in some colleagues with whom I've worked: the good sense to know when it is the right season to hash out a disagreement, and when it is the season to communicate more subtly, or just to "let it be" for a while, to let silence speak. In certain instances, the latter is the better approach. In that silence, there may actually be communication and even healing, or at least a truce being forged. The 13th century Sufi poet Rumi wrote: "There is a channel between voice and presence, a way where information flows. In disciplined silence the channel opens; with wandering talk, it closes." I must remind myself that my inclinations are not always the proper season, the right time, to confront conflict or disagreement. Sometimes, disciplined silence opens a channel of information, communication and even understanding of another's viewpoint.

## What We Can Learn from Conflict

BUT, WAIT A MINUTE – IS CONFLICT ITSELF ALWAYS THE CULPRIT? As Ramsay Clark said, "Turbulence is a life force. It is opportunity. Let's love turbulence and use it for change." That's awfully hard to swallow, I admit, under certain circumstances – maybe when we feel our boss has not supported us on an important issue, or when someone has betrayed us by repeating something we told them in confidence. Rainer Maria Rilke cautioned, "Tell a wise man or remain silent." It's that remaining silent part that gets me on a regular basis. Parker Palmer and Tom VanderArk, in the preface to *Teaching with Fire* note that we live in a society where anger is feared and where our culture encourages us to suppress anger, in case it comes destructive. These authors note, though, that anger when properly expressed may contain healing energy. This anger may be used to creative ends. And if it is suppressed, we may end up depressed. "What better way to protect the status quo than to convince people to tuck away their anger leading them into a depression that deprives them of the will, the energy and the hope for change?" (p. xxi). I have met educators and clinicians who are in this situation. They live with a gnawing, suppressed anger over the conditions of their work, choked by regulations, burdened by the cumbersome system of health insurance, paper work, wasted hours filling out useless forms. Not only is their anger suppressed; what also is suppressed is their creativity, their joy for their vocation because they perceive few if any sources of inspiration.

In 2006 I helped give a series of workshops around the country with several collaborators, including Dr. Catherine Carotta, Associate Director of the Center for Childhood Deafness at Boys Town National Research Hospital in Omaha. Cathy and I first worked together over 20 years ago here in Indiana, after I had moved from Omaha, so our paths have criss-crossed, or maybe I should say they are interwoven like Celtic knots. Cathy's contribution to our workshops was a marvelous section on working within a team to better serve children with special needs. She introduced us to the concepts from *Five Dysfunctions of a Team*, one of the most important of which is that conflict, in and of itself, is not a bad thing. According to this method, the goal should not be to get rid of conflict without resolution, but to put conflict on the table, treat it honestly and with respect, and come to some agreement about how differences will be approached – even if the answer is to agree to disagree.

## Loving vs. Liking Others

THE FACT REMAINS THERE ARE SOME PEOPLE WE LIKE MORE THAN OTHERS. There are some people I've worked with whom I'd give anything to work with again, and others whom I really don't miss at all. I examine my own feelings about the latter group - Do I harbor ill feelings toward these people? I'd like to think I don't. Yet, as Catherine of Genoa wrote, "From time to time I feel that I am growing only to see that I have a long way to go." We're not required to embrace everyone with whom we work. A theologian as great as C.S. Lewis was clear on that one! "Kindness is within our power," wrote Samuel Johnson, "even when fondness is not." We are required, I believe to a) see every person as a child of God and therefore precious and deserving of respect and dignity; and b) examine our negative feelings, when they arise, to understand their source. What does my dislike of this person, or my conflict with him or her say about me? What are my motives in this? My fears? Why am I letting hostility control me?

When I am in conflict with a colleague, I remember the words of Walt Whitman that began this chapter, and that inspired the title of Lloyd C. Douglass' classic book *Disputed Passage*. These words give me pause every time because they chastise me to examine myself, not to point a finger at others: "Have you not learned great lessons from those who braced themselves against you and disputed the passage with you?" I've thought about this a lot after reading *Gilead*. I loved Robinson's thoughts on our interactions with others. When we encounter another person, we might ask ourselves, "What is God wanting of me in this experience, in this moment?" This is really true when this "other person" disagrees with us or is hostile, critical or threatening. We do not like to have our authority questioned or our ego deflated. That's hard on our, uh, well, our ego. Kula, in *Yearnings* notes that we may be resistant to talking out problems with colleagues, because most of us really don't want to be convinced that we're wrong. Kula says we have to fight that defensiveness to hang on to our position for dear life, I know I do. He says, "If you allow [another's] point of view to sit beside your own, it's incredible how you and the situation can be transformed" (p. 9). That transformation may only take place if, as St. Benedict said, we "listen with the ears of our heart."

## Wisdom from the Old Testament

*I've read something from the Old Testament that I would do well TO remember. The story in I Kings 21:17 (RSV) that tells how the Lord sent the prophet Elijah to meet King Ahab who had wronged a citizen named Naboth. When Elijah appeared before Ahab the king cried out, "Have you found me, O my enemy?" Elijah was the enemy not to the person of the king but to the king's greed and cruelty. Sometimes when we are in conflict, the other person is an opponent only because he or she brings us face to face with our own*

*attitudes and views, not because that person is our enemy or sees us as one. We may have conflict with another person who truly respects us as a person or a professional but disagrees with our position. Our mistake, however, is sometimes to return hostility to the other person and not to that person's views. After all, the other person could be right! How hard this is to navigate when we are hurting from being opposed.*

MARILYNNE ROBINSON IN *GILEAD* NOTES, "IF YOU CONFRONT INSULT OR antagonism, your first impulse will be to respond in kind. But if you think, as it were, this is an emissary sent from the Lord, and some benefit is intended for me, first of all the occasion to demonstrate my faithfulness, the chance to show that I do in some small degree participate in the grace that saved me, you are free to act otherwise than as circumstances would seem to dictate. You are free to act by your own lights. He [the person with whom you are in conflict] would probably laugh at the thought that the Lord sent him to you for your benefit (and his), but that is the perfection of the disguise, his own ignorance of it" (p. 124).

## Gossip and Its Destructive Effects

I CAN'T LEAVE THE CONCEPT OF CONFLICT AMONG CO-WORKERS WITHOUT MENtioning gossip – a behavior that at times is just an innocent outlet of steam. We vent our frustrations with one colleague about another, and then feel better, and that is that. Right? But, there is a more insidious form of gossip that can permeate a workplace. Gossip can have an alluring effect that draws us in and if we don't resist, before we know it, we have participated in mean-spirited behavior whose effects may have far-reaching and damaging consequences. I have been guilty of this. I have also watched in admiration as a few of my colleagues, especially my friend, Julia, practice the art of just not responding when gossip is mentioned, refusing to be part of it. The recent Broadway play, *Doubt*, has as its sobering, central theme the insidious effects of unsubstantiated rumor. A priest character in the play gives a sermon that tells the same classic story found in the poem, "The Monk and the Peasant" by Margaret E. Bruner, reprinted at the end of this chapter.

Gossip, like envy and other emotions, is really a derivative of jealousy. It would be easy to bring these Thursday thoughts to an end by skirting these themes of Jealousy and Gossip, but I feel the need to pitch them in for my own sake. Even though we are professionals, I know in our work with children and their families that we have to deal with jealousy. We are jealous of a colleague who receives special recognition. We experience that emotion if one among us does an outstanding thing, has his or her name highlighted in publications, earns a good deal more money than we do or who receives credit for something we think we deserved. Jealousy is a human emotion, deeply rooted in ambition and insecurities. We all experience it in some way at some time or the other.

## The Green-Eyed Monster

**O**F COURSE JEALOUSY DOES IRREPARABLE HARM TO OUR WORK AND TO OUR relationships and we need to be constantly on guard against it and its effects. It so dramatically highlights weakness in our own self esteem. It will always be true as Iago declared, "Jealousy, my Lord, is a green-eyed monster that mocks the meat it feeds on," and "The beauty of your life makes me feel ugly."

Yes, I have dealt with jealousy in my life and work. Even as I write this I know I am not above thinking I've done better than someone else who was recognized and I wasn't. I know how easy it is for me to claim someone got ahead because of favoritism rather than hard work. And then I hear in my head words from John Baillie's Evening prayer for the Second Day, asking God for forgiveness for, "....my unwillingness to believe you have called me to a small work and my brother to a great one."

We would learn a great deal about ourselves that we would resent if someone else were bluntly honest with us. But, if I have the courage to look deep into the mirror of my soul I know I will see there the effects of ambition, of too much pride, of an over-active ego. I know firsthand how easy it is to be so involved in achieving that I forget about my first task which is to become a whole person where I can truly "rejoice with those who rejoice." I must not stray too far from what James wrote in his New Testament letter. "For where jealousy and selfish ambition exist there will be disorder" (3:16).ev

## Eating our Words

**A**ND WHILE I'M AT IT, I MUST MENTION ANOTHER FORM OF CONFLICT - THE criticism we feel entitled or justified to express when observing the actions of others. In my case, I can do this with a self-righteousness that is uncharitable. How I regret some criticisms and unkind words I have expressed about others. My friend, Maureen, says that when she and her siblings were growing up and would criticize other people by saying, "I'd never do that!" her mother would say, "Do you know why I'm so heavy? It's because of all of my own words over the years that I've had to eat!" In my case, I've eaten enough of my own words to constitute a veritable banquet.

*Maybe those blue jays over the lawn aren't just playing games after all, maybe they're shouting proud words at one another, involved in a situation of jealousy, or just maybe they are working it out, talking it out, making peace in the middle of their controversy. I don't know. But I do know I need to examine my own feelings, the state of my relationship with my colleagues and to clear my life and conscience of whatever jealousy is there to hinder those relationships.*

*I think God wants me to do this, to do it often, and to do it so I can be free of such an unnecessary burden.*

## Forgiveness

BUT WHAT IF THAT INCLUDES FORGIVING OTHERS FOR UNKIND WORDS OR deeds, unfair treatment in the workplace or hurtful insinuations or a host of other unpleasant behaviors? I appreciate the reverent yet pragmatic thoughts of Henri J. M. Nouwen in his *Bread for the Journey* devotional book. In one daily reading about forgiveness called, "How Time Heals" Nouwen disputes the claim that time always heals, particularly if we simply bury hurt feelings and ignore reality. He notes that time does heal when our charitable and authentic actions in a difficult relationship lead us to a deeper understanding of the ways we have hurt each other. In these cases, Nouwen says, "'Time heals' implies not sitting passively but dealing actively with our hurt and trusting the possibility of forgiveness and reconciliation." On top of it all, forgiving others is as much in OUR interest as in the interest of the person needing our forgiveness. Anne Lamott wrote in one of her books that not forgiving another person is like taking rat poison and expecting the rat to die. We only hurt ourselves when we deny forgiveness. Reinhold Niebuhr summed it up, "Forgiveness is the final form of love."

I read recently of an almost unimaginable act of profound forgiveness. In 2006, Charles Roberts opened fire in an Amish schoolhouse, killing many children and leaving three young girls severely and permanently disabled. The Amish committee that has received donations from around the world published an accounting on the one-year anniversary of the shooting, noting how these donations were being distributed. Included in the list of recipients of some of the donated money are the widow and children of Charles Roberts, the man who murdered the Amish children. There are few greater acts of human forgiveness that I can envision.

## The Walls Come Tumblin' Down

WELL, NOW IT'S TIME FOR ME TO STEP BACK AND LET GOD'S GIFT OF THIS season turn me away from outer things to inner things. As always music helps me do this, God's music. So many powerful words to hymns were written by Isaac Watts including "O God, Our Help in Ages Past," and "Joy to the World." I love Watts' hymn, "I Sing the Almighty Power of God," especially the third verse. "There's not a plant or flower below, but makes Your glories known, And clouds arise, and tempests blow, by order from Your throne. While all that borrows life from Thee is ever in Your care, and everywhere that we can be, Thou, God, art present there."

# My Own Worst Enemy

I'VE GOT TO POUND INTO MY BRAIN AND ESPECIALLY MY HEART THE TRUTH that in all the blowing of tempests of conflict and disagreement both my antagonism and myself are in God's care. I may be tempted to think I'm more in His care than my antagonist but that's foolish to the point of blasphemy. It doesn't take Sigmund Freud to tell me I'm often my own worst enemy, a victim of being human. I do good things, I do things less than good. I forgive, I withhold forgiving. I love, sometimes I'm unloving and unlovable. Sometimes I understand perfectly why this person or that person might have a conflict with me. One time in our family when my father was visiting I was having a difficult time with one or more of the boys. I was impatient, I raised my voice, I probably wasn't in the best of moods. When I got up the next morning my father had written out one of his famous notes for members of his family. This note said, "Her voice was ever sweet, gentle, and low, an excellent thing….." Of course he was quoting King Lear in his grief over the death of his daughter, Cordelia." Ouch, Dad! He didn't criticize, he didn't accuse me of being a poor mother, he just reminded me gently of something I needed to hear.

I marvel at how my father is able to give feedback to his children in such a loving and non-threatening way. And, he often sprinkles it with humor, a great disarming tool. I hope I can follow Dad's example when I interact with my own children, and the families with whom I work.

"I think that I shall never see a poem lovely as a tree," or anything as delicate as a snowflake or anything as majestic as an eagle in flight or as beautiful as my children or the sound of rain on the window or the feel of God soaring high above me in the rafters of our church. The peace that comes to me when I've made a friend of an enemy or untangled a tangled relationship or understood the hurts and insecurities behind the conduct of another person is something incomparably sweet. These are the times and moments when I grow a little, deepen a little, mellow a little, thank God a lot.

Such gifts and graces are as predictable as the seasons that come and go. Today I promise myself that I will not be in conflict with that pile of laundry in the basement. That pile of laundry is my opportunity to make something clean. I will take that to heart and try to apply it to my own conduct in this season of God's grace. This seems like a soul-satisfying way for me to bring these Fourth Day thoughts to an end and make way for God's blessings which are just outside my door waiting to greet me. I close my eyes and thank God for Franz Joseph Haydn and all Creation.

*The thing I pray today, again quoting words from a beloved hymn, is that God would "open my eyes that I might see, glimpses of truth thou hast for me…….." Or, the words from the third verse of that hymn:*

> *"Open my mouth, and let me bear gladly the*
> *warm truth everywhere;*
> *Open my heart and let me prepare love with thy*
> *children thus to share.*
> *Silently now, I wait for thee, ready, my God, thy*
> *will to see.*
> *Open my heart, illumine me, Spirit divine!*

*I close my journal with, "And there was morning and there was evening, the fourth day."*

# RESOURCES FOR RE-CREATION WITHIN CONFLICT

## Individual Resources:

1. When working with parents: Read Carolyne Edwards' sensitive essay "Reflections on Counseling" an issue of *Loud & Clear* newsletter available on-line at www.bionicear.com

2. The practical techniques from three resources about conflict may be helpful when dealing with patients and their families, with colleagues, or within our personal relationships. These are: *How to Disagree without being Disagreeable* by Suzette Haden Elgin, Ph.D.; *The Five Dysfunctions of a Team* by Patrick Lencioni; and *The Six Thinking Hats* by Edward De Bono.

3. O'Donohue (p. 17) quotes Blaise Pascal, "In difficult times you should always carry something beautiful in your mind. Go back to nature to find serenity and a sense of divine order, as Rilke advised, "During hard times, stay close to one simple thing in nature. When the mind is festering with trouble or the heart torn, we can find healing among the silence of mountains or fields or listen to the simple steadying rhythm of waves. The slowness and stillness gradually take us over......When we go out among nature, clay is returning to clay. We are returning to participate in the stillness of the earth which first dreamed us." How can you put these ideas into practice?

4. Walk a labyrinth with a stone in your pocket that symbolizes a burden you are carrying, perhaps unpleasant discord with a colleague or family member. When you reach the center, place the stone there, symbolizing the letting go of this burden from the load you carry. Your step is lighter, physically and spiritually, as you walk your way from the center to the end of the labyrinth.

## Group Resources:

1. Read the following passage, adapted from "Managing From the Heart" by Hyler Bracey. How could the messages expressed improve colleagues' abilities to work alongside one another?

*Hear and understand me.*

> *When people feel they have been listened to and understood,*
> *they will be ready to hear what the manager has to say.*

*Even if you disagree, please don't make me wrong.*

> *People resent having their self-worth questioned.*
> *If they don't get mad, they get even.*

*Acknowledge the greatness within me.*

> *Everyone has the potential to grow; people tend to*
> *respond positively when that potential for great-*
> *ness is recognized.*

*Remember to look for my loving intentions.*

> *Recognize positive motivations.*

*Tell me the truth with compassion.*

> *Talk to people respectfully, not about them dis-*
> *dainfully.*

2. Discuss the effect this passage from John Baillie's *Diary of Private Prayer*, "Second Day Evening" has on you:

> *"I ask forgiveness for......*
> *My failure to be true even to my own accepted standards;*
> *My self-deception in the face of temptation;*
> *My choosing of the worse when I know the better;*
> *My complacence towards wrongs that do not touch my*
> *own case and my over-sensitiveness to those that do;*
> *My hardness of heart towards my neighbors' faults and my*
> *readiness to make allowance for my own;*
> *My unwillingness to believe you have called me to a small*
> *work and my brother [or sister] to a great one."*

3. Share with the group your completion of the sentence: "I have effectively dealt with conflict by.............."

4. Have you experienced the destructive nature of gossip in your workplace? Read and talk about the relevance of this poem to your experiences:

> *The Monk and The Peasant by Margaret E. Bruner*

> *A peasant once unthinkingly*
> *Spread tales about a friend.*
> *But later found the rumors false*

*And hoped to make amend.*
*He sought the counsel of a monk,*
*A man esteemed and wise,*
*Who heard the peasant's story through*
*And felt he must advise.*
*The kind monk said:*
*"If you would have*
*A mind again at peace,*
*I have a plan whereby you may*
*From trouble find release.*
*"Go fill a bag with chicken down*
*And to each dooryard go*
*And lay one fluffy feather where*
*The streams of gossip flow.*
*The peasant did as he was told*
*And to the monk returned,*
*Elated that his penance was*
*A thing so quickly earned.*
*"Not yet," the old monk sternly said,*
*"Take up your bag once more*
*And gather up the feathers that*
*You placed at every door.*
*The peasant, eager to atone,*
*Went hastening to obey,*
*No feathers met his sight, the wind*
*Had blown them all away."*

# THE FIFTH DAY

RE-CREATION OF
INSPIRATION

*So God created the great sea monsters and every
living creature that moves, with which the waters
swarm according to their kinds, and every winged
bird according to its kind. (Gen. 1:20-21)*

*Praise the Lord....mountains and all hills, fruit
trees and all cedars, beasts and all cattle, creeping
things and flying birds.  (Ps.148:9-10)*

*"There is nothing in the world that has the cutting
edge of a new thought. It is fascinating to watch
the clearance it can make and the new life it can
bring. Often, without knowing it, we are waiting for a new idea to come and cut us free from
our entanglement. When the idea is true and
our space is ready for it, the idea overtakes everything....indeed, it becomes the mother of a whole
sequence of new feeling, thinking and action."*
-(O'Donohue, p. 43)

# Life in the Garden

*O goodness, Lord, it's already the fifth day, so much has happened
in this Creation that I've missed. There are so many sounds of life I
haven't heard, so many new blooms I haven't seen, so much laughter I've not been able to enjoy, so many things from the garden I
may not appreciate today. You've done all this creating and I've not
known about half of it. I will say there's a cricket that's managed
to get into my basement who is chirping his little heart out and I
cannot locate him in spite of my best efforts.*

THE ANIMAL KINGDOM, "ALL CREATURES GREAT AND SMALL," PROVIDE SUCH
fascination, even awe, that they fit well for me with today's focus on inspiration. The Latin root of the word inspiration is inspirare, to breathe in, to
draw air into the lungs, to take in fresh air. It occurs to me that by inspiration I
am thinking both of my need to be re-inspired as a therapist, and to my students'
need to be inspired and reinforced for creativity. As I write about this fifth day of
Creation from Genesis I think immediately of our back yard here in Indianapolis.
The "swarms" mentioned in the Bible passage above, and it is with them that I start
the day. Things out there are flying, climbing, crawling, running, jumping and making more noise than the Indianapolis Symphony Orchestra when it's tuning up. I
often take my little patients outside to hear the sounds of nature in our garden, to
listen for the many different bird calls, the rustling of leaves, even the gurgling of
water in our backyard fountain. A young mother and I had a triumphant moment
when her deaf daughter alerted to a new sound a few months after her cochlear implant was first activated. This four-year-old, standing in my back yard, was insistent

on finding the source of a new and strange sound, and we eventually did. It was the chattering, clacking of two squirrels (have you ever heard the sound an irritated squirrel makes?) carrying on what seemed to be a heated discussion of some kind.

## All Things Bright and Beautiful

THE WINGED, FURRY, SMOOTH-SKINNED, LONG, SHORT, BIG, SMALL CREATURES have a life of their own and I am not privy to what they say to one another or to me or what their plans are for the day. I suspect they have schedules just like I do. There may be conspiracies going on out there for all I know. What I do know is that I love these creatures, admire and appreciate them, and do the most I can to provide for them (ok, let's keep the mosquitoes out of this) and thank God he saw fit to provide for the creation of the several thousands of species of animal life that share this planet with us humans. I think it would be a very dreary place without these hummingbirds that flutter so effortlessly (effortlessly as far as I know) just a few feet away from my sight here. On my top-10 list of favorite hymns is, "All Things Bright and Beautiful" that declares:

> "All things bright and beautiful
> All creatures great and small;
> All things wise and wonderful
> The Lord God made them all."

The words to this hymn were written by a 19th century Irish woman, Cecil Frances Alexander. Part of her publishing success was due to the fact that virtually no one knew she was a woman because of her name. Alexander composed over 400 poems and hymns for children compiled in the book, "Hymns for Little Children." She wrote that she was originally trying to explain the Apostle's Creed to children when it came to her that she should do so in a way that rhymed, and she was inspired to write the beautiful poem, "All Creatures Great and Small." Can it be coincidence – no, it must be synchronicity – that Cecil Frances Alexander had a passion for helping deaf children? The money earned from her first publications helped build the Derry and Raphoe Diocesan Institution for the Deaf in Strabane, Ireland, and all her subsequent profits were donated to this school. We sing a 17th century melody to those words in our hymnal, but I prefer the lovely tune written by the English contemporary composer, John Rutter. In the morning I occasionally go to a website that displays Alexander's words and has the Rutter accompaniment playing as background music. Sometimes, I sing the hymn aloud. On this fifth day of Re-Creation, I did just that, and actually, can think of no better morning prayer.

## Learning to Like Animals

I HAVE TO SAY THAT AS A CHILD I WAS NOT AN ANIMAL LOVER BY NATURE OR by instinct. I left the hugging of cats and kissing of dogs to my two sisters and brother, who were the entire Animal Rescue and Rehabilitation Society of the State of Nebraska. Celia rescued and then raised a whole litter of bunnies whose mother had been killed by our neighbor's cat, Tuffo; she brought baby birds into the house in shoe boxes when they'd been pushed out of the nest by their mothers. My brother, Joel, had a pair of rats who would actually snuggle and cuddle with him and respond uniquely to his voice, always making me think of Curly's line in "Oklahoma," that "…….he treated the rats like equals." My siblings taught me. I had to learn to touch a frog or stroke a pet rat or not gag when one of my sisters let a lizard crawl on her face when we lived in Panama. But I did learn from them about all creatures great and small, and I'm glad I did because now, on this Friday morning, when I read from this text from the Creation story I know what the lizard knows: a friendly face is a friendly place to feel at home.

## New Questions to Ask

ON THIS FIFTH DAY, I'M THINKING ABOUT THE RE-CREATION OF INSPIRATION in our professional lives. I know one of the reasons I've "kept on a-goin'," as Grandma Ocie said, in this profession is because I've been lucky enough to find new sources of inspiration, new technology to use with patients and some new questions to ask. Irwin Kula, in *Yearnings* quotes his mother as saying, "When you've got an answer, it's time to find better questions" (p. 3). I don't think there's a clinician among us who doesn't want that newness of idea - it brings our vocational commitment alive again or at least revives a weakened battery. Maybe, as is often described, new sources and ideas feel like a breath of fresh air.

## My Own Backyard

WHEN I OPENED THE SMALL PRIVATE PRACTICE IN MY HOME TEN YEARS ago, it was the first time I had worked in a non hospital/clinic setting, and that change meant I could take my patients outside during part of our therapy session. What an inspiration that was, an unexpected revelation of new activities and possibilities suddenly presented themselves. How much more the children could learn and absorb when we could explore, for instance, the bulging tunnels a mole had dug in my flowerbed overnight, (much to my husband's dismay I might add) or discover the crunching sound that walking on snowdrifts makes. For classroom teachers who take their students outside everyday these things probably seem mundane, like a normal part of the educational experience. But for a speech-language pathologist focusing primarily on children with hearing loss who was accustomed to working in an intervention room and "therapizing" with objects or even pictures, the availability of nature and the opportunities in my backyard represented a new source of inspiration for me. This was especially exciting with my particular patients who are learning each day to listen to and interpret the sounds of the world. I think every clinician wishes for that new inspiration but must find it in his or her own time and place. For me, a few years back, it was in my own backyard. Thinking back to that time, I can relate to the words of Nevin Compton Trammell's poem (reprinted in its entirety at the end of this chapter) "I'm Tired, I'm Whipped":

> *I'm working hard*
> *to find truth*
> *in my own backyard…..*

I am one of those of my generation who grew up with *The Wizard of Oz*. A generation or two have grown up with that wonderful movie since my childhood and probably other generations will grow up with it too. It's just one of those films that never lose its appeal. It is a wonderful memory of mine on the Sunday night that it was shown on television then, perhaps once a year in the 1960's, when our family would gather around our old TV set. Mom would have treats and hot chocolate and we would all be transported back in time, or forward in time maybe, to the magical Land of Oz. Like other movies we see and books we read we can remember over time certain things said or events happened that impress on our minds and memories. For me, among all the magical memories of that movie which I still watch when it comes on today is the final scene when Dorothy sums up her experience with Toto. About the last thing she says is, "If I ever go looking for my heart's desire again and can't find it in my own backyard, well then I probably never lost it to begin with." What Dorothy calls, "My heart's desire," I suppose, is my vocation. How could I known then that, all these years later, it would be there in my very own back yard where I would find a whole host of sources for creative renewal in my work?

## Dust Can Clog Windows and Enthusiasm

THE RELATIVELY SMALL CHANGE OF BEING ABLE TO TAKE MY LITTLE CHARGES outside opened a whole new avenue of ideas for teaching that had never been available to me. I know I need these new surges in order to be re-vitalized and, therefore, re-inspired to stick with my work and my commitments to families. Maybe that's in all of us. I suspect it is – and I know writers have discussed this for time and eternity. As the hymn says, "Breathe on me, breath of God. Fill me with life anew." John O'Donohue has a passage that makes me think of times when my professional role seemed stagnant, monotonous, repetitive and uncreative. Because of the nature of our work and the energy it requires of us, if we aren't periodically inspired, aren't sometimes infused with passion for a new project, we can begin to feel empty and our jobs mechanical. O'Donohue writes: "If a house is closed for a long time, dust clogs the windows. The same thing can happen in the rooms of the mind. If one has become stuck in a certain narrow or predictable way of seeing, the outside light cannot bring color into one's life …the outside world loses its invitation and challenge. When no fresh light can come into the mind, the color and beauty fade from light" (p. 18).

## Surprised by Light

AMONG THE MANY SONGS OF MY FAITH THAT I LOVE IS ONE WITH HAYDN'S music and words by Cowper, "Sometimes a Light Surprises." When I sing this hymn I have the same feeling Helen Keller must have had when in moments of great inspiration she is reported to have "seen" in color. I never quite believed this until Chris Barton, a composer and my music therapy colleague who is not blind told me that ever since she was a little girl she has seen corresponding colored lights that accompany musical notes and patterns as she composes music in her head. (For the record, Chris says the scientific term for the triggering of two senses simultaneously is synaesthesia.) I don't see lights when I hear certain hymns, but I do feel the music resonate within me:

> "Sometimes a light surprises the Christian while she sings
> It is the Lord who rises with healing in his wings.
> When comforts are declining he grants the soul again
> A season of clear shining to cheer it after rain."

One of the joys of life, certainly of the wonders of life, is that these moments of surprise come at the most unexpected times. Is it really possible that we can sing when we don't feel like singing, that the singing itself lifts us up from the dark mood of overwork, disappointments and worries? "How shall we sing the songs of the Lord in a strange land?" asked the writer of Psalm 137. To the mind-boggling renewal of the spirit through the ages the discovery has been made that after rainy days there flows always a season of clear shining.

My father's father, a physician, after a lifetime of overwork and disappointments, suffered the loss of much of his emotional stability. But my father's mother tells how in some of her husband's darkest moods he would sing hymns which he remembered from his childhood. My father has little doubt that his singing in those dark times were a part of his father's discovery of the Lord rising with healing, that in his times of rain the light was a light of surprises.

## Sponge, Funnel, Strainer or Sieve

WHEN OUR FAMILY LEFT PANAMA TO MOVE BACK TO THE U.S., A FAMIly friend, Rabbi Jacques Reese gave us a little book titled, *Ethics of the Fathers* by Philip Birnbaum. In one of these collected sayings there is a quotation that has special meaning for me as I think about my continuing quest for inspiration in my work. It is one of the many sayings from the wisdom of the

Jewish faith:

> *There are four types of those who sit in the presence of the sages: the sponge, the funnel, the strainer and the sieve. The sponge absorbs all, the funnel receives at one end and spills out at the other, the strainer lets the wine through and retains the dregs, the sieve lets out the flour dust and retains the fine flour.*

I'm not sure sometimes where I am exactly when it comes to the spiritual life. I know, like the funnel, I let lots of God's inspiration spill out in waste, I just don't always respond to what God is saying to me. I try to be like the sieve – making use of what is useful and not letting the best of God's inspiration go to waste. I don't always do this perfectly by any means (you'd be surprised how often I completely waste a rainbow) but I do try as I learn and grow.

## *Music Comes To My Practice*

I'M THINKING OF ANOTHER EXAMPLE OF NEW INSPIRATION THAT HAS COME INTO my practice. It came serendipitously when I had run out of ideas about how to work with a severely multiply-involved deaf child. I called Chris Barton, whom I mentioned earlier, to see if she would observe a session and give me some ideas. I knew Chris as my children's former music teacher and composer of children's folk music, but also knew she was a licensed music therapist and had worked previously with special-needs children. Chris answered my desperate summons that day, and she….well…..she worked her magic is the only way I can describe it. She worked it on my little patient and on his mother, who was probably losing faith in my ability to make any headway with her son. Suddenly, this child was clapping and rocking to music, making at least fleeting eye contact, engaged and interested for the first time! And Chris worked her magic on me. As the poet e.e. cummings wrote, "….now the ears of my ears awake and now the eyes of my eyes are opened…." And that's how I felt. I had never seen the power of music demonstrated so convincingly and I knew that day it was going to open a whole new, untapped resource for my students. I certainly understand that many other clinicians already knew this and were implementing it. My point is that on that day with Chris, I became open to the possibility of music as a genuine, and for some children essential, means of communication, not just a fun, added-on, only-if-we-have-extra-time activity. Since then, Chris and I have co-treated many children, published an integrated speech/ music therapy program, and collaborated on projects together. We have a relationship, as many of you do with certain colleagues that is a sort of soul connection. We can finish each others' sentences. We can work together with a child and his parent and seamlessly integrate our two lesson plans without prior discussion. When we later discovered that we actually share the same birthday, we felt our status as soul sisters was justified.

## Inspiration and Surprises in Many Forms

I've MENTIONED HOW NEW INSPIRATION, BREATHS OF FRESH AIR, CAME TO ME when I found music to be a partner with speech therapy or when I had access to nature in my backyard, but don't mean to imply that everyone will find his or her inspiration there - probably not my colleague, Susan, who lives on the 18th floor of a high rise in Manhattan. But, she and I both saw the same picture on the front page of the *New York Times* on September 14, 2004. It showed a group of children being greeted by their new teacher on the first day of school at P.S. 75 in Manhattan. While most of the children have a fairly cool expression, perhaps of wariness, the face of one boy in the front of the group, with his big brown eyes, and a smile as wide as the sky, stands out among the crowd. He looks up eagerly to see his new teacher – his excitement is palpable. Susan and I called each other that morning, "Did you see that little boy's face on the front page? Now that's the face of a child who can bring new inspiration to even a worn-out teacher." As I looked at that child's expression, I thought of Lewis Carroll's Prologue to *Looking Glass*, "Child of the pure unclouded brow and dreaming eyes of wonder....." I still keep that picture from the newspaper on my messy office-door bulletin board to remind me of the excitement of children and their "dreaming eyes of wonder."

## Inspiration in the Yorkshire Moors

THE LITERARY WORKS OF THE BRONTE SISTERS ALWAYS HAVE INTRIGUED me, especially when considering the rich abundance of their imaginative ideas and the conditions of their upbringing. I had the chance to learn of their extraordinary lives during the year I spent at Leeds University in Yorkshire, England, between my undergraduate and graduate studies. The Bronte family lived in Yorkshire in the early-to-mid 19th century. During their short lives, Charlotte, Emily and Anne Bronte each wrote a novel, *Wuthering Heights*, *Jane Eyre* and *Agnes Grey*, respectively, that is considered a classic in English literature. From Leeds, I could make the short trip to Haworth, the village in the Yorkshire moors where the three sisters and their brother, Branwell lived after their father became curate there. In the parsonage that was their home, one can still see the creativity and inspiration all four children had, even at very early ages. Still preserved, 150 years later, are books no bigger than match boxes with original stories and drawings sketched out in such tiny handwriting that a magnifying glass is required to read them.  In what were isolated and seemingly dreary surroundings, these siblings managed to find source after source of inspiration for their writings, something that I must admit, baffles me.

The three sisters were also talented poets and jointly published a volume of verse using androgynous pseudonyms.  Charlotte, Emily and Anne Bronte, barely in their 20's, published their poems under the names Currer, Ellis and Acton Bell to avoid the prejudice against female writers. Emily Bronte's poem, "To Imagination", is an ode to inspiration in which she addresses Imagination directly, as one would a friend:

> But thou art ever there to bring
> The hovering vision back, and breathe
> New glories o'er the blighted spring
> And call a lovelier life from death,
> And whisper of a voice divine
> Of real worlds as bright as thine.

Only two copies of the Bronte's book of poems were sold. Undeterred, the sisters continued to create, to imagine and to be inspired, even in the often bleak conditions of their real lives. Did they turn inward for their inspiration? Or to each other? Two years ago, Jane, a colleague in Yorkshire and her husband, Ian, made the trek with me back to Haworth when I was working near there. On a snowy February day, the three of us walked in and around the parsonage that still looks almost as it would have all those years ago. My own imagination took flight as I again read Emily's poem in the book of verse that now sells many copies under the Bronte's real names. Imagination, ".....breathes new glories o'er the blighted spring and calls a lovelier life......" Where shall I continue to search for new ideas in my work that will call my students and me toward "a lovelier life?"

## No Perfect Job

A COLLEAGUE WHO HAS FOUND HERSELF IN A RUT PROFESSIONALLY TOLD ME recently, "It's easy for you to come up with new ideas and inspirations, you have a private practice, you can choose or reject any patient or project that comes along. I am, on the other hand, stuck in a school district or a bureaucratic institution where creativity isn't rewarded or even encouraged." I considered her comment and replied that yes, she was right, and no, she was wrong! I have worked twice as many years in large medical centers as I have in my home-based private practice, so I do know the constraints of big institutions. I also know there is room for creativity, sources of inspiration, and the potential for renewed vigor and new ideas, though I readily admit you may have to do more convincing in order to be supported in your efforts, or to work around your institutional schedule, to make room for inspirational possibilities. Regardless of your work venue one thing about inspiration is that you have to create some open spaces for it in the busyness of everyday life. You can't schedule it, as in, "Okay, at 2:00 this afternoon I'm going to be inspired," but you do have to make room for periods of reflection away from the phone and the ubiquitous email to protect those periods. Only then will you be present if inspiration does appear. Like a fickle house guest, there's no guaranteeing that inspiration will show up at the appointed hour, but at least she's been invited, and who knows when she may arrive? I find that I write best when I let my mind escape to the place that is just removed from my present surroundings. No, I'm not in a trance, but I do feel my most productive writing times are when I am "somewhere else," absent in a way, from the immediate world around me. Only then can I search deep enough inside me to find my center, and my words. The Chilean poet, Vicente Huidobro wrote, "I am absent, but deep in this absence there is the waiting for my-self; and this waiting is another form of presence; the waiting for my return."

I'll add as an aside and a reality check that anyone who has a romanticized view of the ideal job as a single practitioner would be sorely disappointed to see how much of what I do now is very mundane precisely because I am completely on my own in my office. I am the one who searches frantically for a misplaced document. It is I, not a technical support person, who fights the paper jams in my printer, I almost lose my religion spending half an hour trying different sequences of numbers to fax something to Italy....you get the picture. I chuckled to read Parker Palmer's description of his home office where, as a single practitioner with no staff, even he experiences some of the frustrations that I do. I took a bit of comfort in that.

## Inspiration from Creatures Great and Small

IT SEEMS MORE AND MORE CLEAR THAT INSPIRATION, NEW IDEAS, NEW PLANS that make us excited to get back to work and try something different, happen when we are doing what we are meant to do with our lives. I write in my journal on this 5th Day when God created all the animal kingdom, and I think about what that means – there is no better example of "doing what you're meant to do" than the amazing creatures God has created. My colleague, Dave Sindrey reminds me of this when he says that a tortoise, odd as he may look, is perfect for what he needs to be. None of us can do everything – but if you're built for running, run; if you're built for teaching, teach; if you're built for flying, you must fly!

## Bless the Beasts and the Children

I OFTEN USE MATERIALS AND TEXTS ABOUT ANIMALS FOR THERAPY ACTIVITIES, whether we're working on reading comprehension, articulation, or vocabulary development. If the content of what children are covering is interesting, the children will be motivated, and if they are motivated, my job, our job, is at least 50% easier. One of my nine-year old students, Leo, with dyslexia, struggles and fights with the printed word but will work willingly to read passages about fascinating examples from the animal kingdom. And, not only is he inspired to keep trying hard, I am much more interested because the animal kingdom is such an amazing source of inspiration. I think of two passages Leo and I read together recently that illustrate this. The first was a description of a wolf spider that creates a hole in the ground and spins a web to line the inside of the hole. Then he creates a lid, complete with a fully-functioning hinge that the spider has spun. Unsuspecting prey fall into the hole and the spider, hiding inside, operates the hinge, closing the trap door and, well, enjoying his lunch. Of course, that's an example of survival of the fittest, the food chain in the animal kingdom and this topic generates a great deal of interesting discussion on its own.

The second example is one of mutual co-existence among creatures. The article Leo and I read was about a type of moth who alights on the neck of a sleeping bird and drinks its tears as the bird slumbers on, completely unaware. A close-up color photograph accompanied this article in *National Geographic* and we could clearly see the moth resting on the sleeping bird's back, with a long skinny protrusion, essentially a drinking straw, emerging from the moth's mouth. The moth slips the straw under the bird's closed eyelid and drinks its tears for half an hour. Leo read that the moth gets a supply of salt and proteins this way, without doing any harm to the bird. Reading this passage was an example of what was mentioned in the opening quote, that new ideas become the mother of a whole new sequence of ideas. This has been true in Leo's case, as he went on to read of many other "tear sippers" in nature, to find articles in books and on-line, and has now committed to doing his Science Fair project on this topic.

## Unexpected Inspiration

THE THING ABOUT THE WONDERFUL WAYS IN WHICH WE ARE INSPIRED AND renewed is that, like Paul on the road to Damascus, it comes even when we may resist it. "Where shall I go to avoid your Spirit?" asks the writer of Psalm 139, 'or how shall I flee from your presence? If I ascend to heaven you are there. If I make my bed in the depths, you are there. If I take the wings of the morning and dwell in the uttermost parts of the sea, even there your hand shall lead me and I shall be held by you." A surprise isn't a surprise unless it really surprises us and just as C.S. Lewis was surprised by joy so you and I can be surprised every day by our patients, by our colleagues, and in our personal lives.

Some of my most rewarding moments of clinical work have come when I least expected them, when they were not part of my stated plan. An example of this is Joey, a deaf four year boy on the severe end of the autism spectrum. He never made eye contact with me for the first two months we worked together, was emotionally-disregulated most of the time, laughing one moment, then crying as if feeling terrorized the next. If I put any pressure on him at all, he would make himself vomit. I never saw him in those early days of our relationship relate to another human being meaningfully. Never. Not through touch, communication or eye contact. One day, as he left our session, my next patient was arriving. She was Holly, a four-month old baby, just fitted with hearing aids, and her mother was carrying her in an infant seat. Holly's mother had set the seat on the sidewalk in order to ring the doorbell, just as Joey, his mother and I walked out the front door and encountered them. Joey ran straight over to the baby, and I had a sudden dread that he might do something to frighten or even harm her. But do you know what that previously detached, isolated, emotionless four-year old boy did? He knelt on the ground, and began cooing and jargoning in a high pitched, soothing "motherese" voice. He reached into the baby seat and stroked Holly's tiny hands. Joey's mother and I were dumb-struck. I never could have constructed a therapy activity that would have elicited that unplanned, genuine expression of affection from Joey.

## Surprises and the Beginner's Mind

I LIKE THE CONCEPT OF THE "BEGINNER'S MIND" THAT PAUL BRENNER USES. Brenner says that when we have the attitude of a beginner's mind, we see a state where possibilities spring eternal – a place where there is actually pleasure and excitement in not knowing everything. I suppose, without really realizing it, I had adopted a "beginner's mind" attitude when I discovered the value of backyard lessons with my patients. Inspiration of all kinds followed and one thing led to another. My colleague Mary Joe's inspiration comes just as naturally from numbers. I remember working in her research lab, and watching her eyes dart across sheets of data collected from deaf children, getting excited and inspired when she saw something that had eluded the rest of us. "Look at these scores," she'd say. "This is amazing. It shows a different pattern than what we had thought. We have to start working immediately on a new measure to tap into this skill." Her mind saw and still sees data sets as things of beauty, as surely as my music therapy colleague, Chris, hears beauty in music and my colleague, Dave, sees and then draws illustrations that bring therapy tasks alive. Each of these colleagues whom I admire is built for something different, and has found the place in this profession where his or her form of creativity may be nurtured.

## Fostering Creativity in Our Clients

THAT BRINGS ME TO ANOTHER SIDE OF CREATIVITY – HOW WE ENCOURAGE creativity in the children with whom we work. I think the first lesson in encouraging creativity is that we have to be flexible enough to abandon the activity we had planned and join into whatever inspires the child right here and now. I had a full lesson planned once for Niko, and was getting a bit anxious about the upcoming testing that would determine his preschool placement, thinking, "We'll spend the session today working on his use of plural endings." But then, as the hymn says, "Sometimes a light surprises," and I opened the door at 8:00 on a sunny autumn morning to find Niko with a rotten apple in his hand. He was much too excited to remember all the social language formalities we normally exchanged, the "Hi, Miss Amy" and so on. Oh no, he launched full throttle into a verbal monologue involving the apple tree in my front yard and how some apples had fallen on the ground and how this particular treasure he held in his hand had a surprise in it: a worm! He insisted I come outside to see the source of these treasures and so his mother and I followed him into the dewy grass (yes, my new leather shoes were getting wet but, oh, well.) The extraordinary thing that stays with me today is that as Niko showed us the apple tree, compared the "good" apples on the tree with the bruised ones on the ground, contrasted the red ones with those that were still green, delighted in the inching-along movements of the tiny white worm in the apple, he pointed all this out as if he thought I had never noticed I had a 30-foot apple tree growing in my front yard. But isn't that the way with inspiration? When it arrives, it is so exciting, usually so unexpected, we want to share it with others and we may feel we are the first ones ever to have seen it. The other memory that stays with me about that experience is  that the words of Robert Frost's poem "Unharvested" were running through my head, reminding me that there is sweetness and joy when events occur that actually interfere with our carefully-laid plans. As Niko, his mother and I found treasure after treasure on the dewy ground that morning, I became aware of the gift of unexpected inspiration.

## Teachable Moments

OF COURSE TALENTED EDUCATORS HAVE BEEN CAPITALIZING ON JUST THESE sorts of teachable moments forever. And for my money, no one handles such moments better than my colleague, Chris Barton. Doing music therapy with Leo, a five-year old boy on the autism spectrum, Chris found that his obsessive interest was in dinosaurs, and in the preying of bigger animals on smaller ones. Chris went right along with this, and, with Leo's help, wrote the song, "I'm a big T-Rex" that is featured on our *TuneUps* CD program of integrated speech and music therapy. The song is so different from every other one in our program and we've received much feedback about how it was the first song that really appealed to certain children, especially boys. I wonder if that is because Chris chose a male friend of hers to record it who has a gravelly, deep bass voice that is, therefore highly audible to children with hearing loss and frankly, a bit spooky! Only the grasping of a teachable moment by a teachable clinician brought that song into existence. Leo's mother says that he has now generalized this idea-turned-to-song by changing the animals in each verse, or applying the idea to different themes, still singing his heart out. I see Leo's blossoming in this case as another illustration of O'Donohue's concept from the beginning of this chapter. The novel idea of a dinosaur song "......became the mother of a whole sequence of new feeling, thinking and action."

## Creating space for inspiration

THE SPARK OF INSPIRATION MIGHT BECOME A FIRE OF ENERGY, OR IT MIGHT burn out. Many factors influence which of these outcomes takes place. I mentioned earlier that inspiration, sometimes to our frustration, needs space and time and can't be forced or over-loaded. Maggie Anderson, a teacher from Montana, writes about this in the poetry anthology, *Teaching with Fire*. "After five years my "fire" was burning brightly. I thrived on the energy that ignites in a classroom. But I was exhausted at the end of the day and overwhelmed by the never-ending list of things to do for my work, my home, my family. After much soul-searching, I realized I was piling on too many logs too tightly and the flame inside me was beginning to wane – even smolder at times. I was desperate for some space. Children need space as well. The constant piling on of facts and figures, the demands of time and energy can quickly douse the flame – the energy that children bring to the classroom. I am learning for myself and for my students, to choose consciously the logs I place on my own fire, and to pay special attention to the spaces that invite reflection and warmth. Given this space between the logs, my students and I often witness the special beauty that ignites and takes on a life of its own" (p. 88). Maggie Anderson then shares the poem, "Fire", by Judy Brown. One of the lines that speaks to me is: "So building fires requires attention to the spaces in between, as much as to the wood."

> *What makes a fire burn*
> *is space between the logs,*
> *a breathing space.*
> *Too much of a good thing,*
> *too many logs*
> *packed in too tight*
> *can douse the flames*
> *almost as surely as a pail of water would.*
>
> *So building fires*
> *requires attention*
> *to the spaces in between,*
> *as much as to the wood.*
>
> *When we are able to build*
> *open spaces*
> *in the same way*
> *we have learned*
> *to pile on the logs,*
> *then we can come to see how*
> *it is fuel, and absence of the fuel*
> *together, that make fire possible.*
>
> *We only need to lay a log*
> *lightly from time to time.*
> *A fire*
> *grows*
> *simply because the space is there,*
> *with openings*
> *in which the flame*
> *that knows just how it wants to burn*
> *can find its way.*
> *-Judy Brown*

# Spaces in Thought, Spaces in the Schedule

M Y DENTIST, MATTHEW, HAS A FASCINATING LIFE AS A FULL-TIME FACULTY member at the Indiana University School of Dentistry (where, for those who are familiar, the father of Howard and William House, world-famous otologists, was dean) and a part-time clinical practice. In what is left of his spare time, he goes to Viet Nam and volunteers for Project Compassion. He's the best dentist I, a former dental phobic, have ever been to. Because he is so good at what he does, I asked him once why he keeps his private practice so small, and he replied, "I couldn't stand the thought of seeing my schedule booked months or even years out with no spaces left for inspiration, new ideas, or the chance to take advantage of opportunities that come along." I know what he means.

*My thoughts this Friday morning are thankfulness for the partial ending of the work week although there are many things left over for the weekend. That's what weekends are for I guess. "Spend the afternoon," writes Annie Dillard. "You can't take it with you." No, I can't, and in the next couple of days, I need time with my family, good friends, with less time pressure and a few moments with the cricket-in-residence that is trying to chirp its way into my affection. (But, no way am I going to pet that creature.) I don't really "weary in well doing" but like you and all the rest of us I do weary. Do crickets weary? I'll ask my siblings, they know all about crickets, I'll probably get a whole hour of cricket lectures from my question.*

*What comes to me in these moments now with the upcoming sun and the down-going moon which was full last night is an over-whelming sense of God's presence that I can almost hear. It's about harmony, creatures living in peace with one another, people living in harmony with one another, human beings living in harmony with the world God has created and provided for, for both humans and animals, for both flora and fauna.*

*As I write on this fifth day about "all creatures great and small," I am reminded of something that is at the heart of God's creative and re-creative powers. Once upon a time, really not more than 100 years ago, the skies of America were filled with the flight of billions of passenger pigeons. Then, because they were slaughtered by the millions, they became extinct. The last passenger pigeon died in 1914 in the Cincinnati zoo. A monument to the passenger pigeon in Wisconsin's Wyaalusing State Park says simply, "This species became extinct through the avarice and thoughtlessness of man."*

# Creativity among Creatures Great and Small

I KNOW I CAN'T BRING BACK THE EXTINCT CARRIER PIGEON BUT CLAY AND I ARE doing our best to make our back yard a sanctuary for every bird who might find its way to central Indiana. During a therapy session with Gina, a three-year old with hearing aids, we took a walk outside in mid-March, as signs of spring were first appearing. The crocuses were blooming, even with a dusting of snow still on the ground! What great fodder for a language lesson, I thought, and kept trying to secure her attention in the flower bed, "Look, Gina…look, a little yellow flower. It's called a crocus. Can you say, "crocus?" But, Gina would have none of it. I'm sure in her mind all she heard was, "blah, blah, blah", because her attention was fully focused on the gas grill on our patio. "How it works?" she wanted to know. "What this thing for?" she persisted. Almost begrudgingly, I abandoned my crocus lesson and we opened the grill. "Sometimes a light surprises!" Believe it or not, a bird, almost surely a robin, had found its way into the grill and had built a nest inside this warm, safe, albeit unusual bird sanctuary. What's more, this inspired bird had adapted to the dimensions of the grill; the nest was rounded on one side and squared off with two perfect corners on the other side, to correspond to the interior space of the grill. Because the nest was as high as the inside of the grill, the mother bird had adjusted by creating the opening at an angle, sort of on the side of the nest. And inside this unusual, creative, shall we say, inspired nest were three light-blue eggs. You can imagine that the rest of the session was spent talking about birds, and nests, and drawing birds and nests, and using all the vocabulary of birds and nests….and, well, I don't think crocuses were ever mentioned again that day.

It was a mild annoyance to Clay and me that we couldn't use our grill during late March and early April, just at the time when it starts becoming fun to cook outside. But, that was a minor inconvenience, and the pay-off came some weeks later when my oldest son, Campbell, came in from the backyard and said, "Mom, I think I hear baby birds chirping inside the gas grill." Don't ask me how, but not only did the baby birds survive (we would peek in on them regularly as they grew), the mother bird had the creativity, the inspiration when the time was right, to get them all out of the grill (I guess they squeezed out the same place she had squeezed in every day) and one day they were gone.

Rachel Carson wrote the classics *Silent Spring* and *The Edge of the Sea*, and warned, long before others were doing so, about the destruction of the environment. The antidote to such destruction, she believed, was to involve children and adults alike in experiencing the inspiration that nature offers us all. In 1954 she said, "The more clearly we can focus our attention on the wonders and realities of the universe about us, the less taste we have for its destruction."

## "Who Has Made All Things Well"

*On this fifth day of Creation I am reminded that God created the passenger pigeon just as he created "every winged bird according to its kind." God did not destroy his own creation in that species, we did. Just as we may destroy through thoughtlessness and neglect these creatures of such beauty so we also may destroy the sources of our own inspiration and renewal. That destruction comes through neglect of the inspiration that is everywhere around us, through spiritual eyes and ears that are closed up against our own re-creation and renewal. And just as surely, it is within our grasp to seize those opportunities for inspiration and renewal, appreciate the creativity of a mother robin, and use those surprises to inspire our patients and be inspired ourselves.*

*How moving, and what a reminder are the words by Cecil Frances Alexander, as I sing the last verse of the hymn "All Creatures Great and Small":*

> *"He gave us eyes to see with*
> *And lips that we might tell*
> *How great is God Almighty*
> *Who has made all things well."*

*I close my journal with, "And there was morning and there was evening, the fifth day."*

# RESOURCES FOR RE-CREATION OF INSPIRATION

## *Individual Resources*

1. Talk to people in your field who are doing work that is creative and really interests you. Ask if you may write or email ideas. I've answered many an email from someone who read an idea of mine and asked me questions about it, requesting permission to re-work or add to my work. Later, they sent me a wonderful spin-off of my idea in which they had applied their own creativity to make the idea even better. This is an example of the quote from the beginning of this chapter: "When an idea is true and our space is ready for it, the idea overtakes everything....indeed, it becomes the mother of a whole sequence of new feeling, thinking and action." Always be careful to fully credit the original source of your work, for their sake and yours.

2. I get inspired when I visit schools and watch teachers teach a lesson with a new twist, something I had never thought of before. Could you trade places for a day with another clinician? You might be amazed at the inspiration that comes from seeing new materials or working in a new space. Similarly, ask someone to observe your work with children, and then observe theirs. A friend said, "I had taught Charlotte's Web a hundred times; then I watched my colleague teach a lesson on that book and was delighted with the new spin she put on things, and how lively the class discussion was. I went back to my class to replicate and build upon her methods. I was more excited to teach the book, and my students felt that excitement and responded in kind with creative and novel ideas."

3. Read the following poem, "I'm Tired, I'm Whipped." Have there been times in your work when, in spite of fatigue or discouragement, you been inspired? Have you "…..somewhere, somehow found your voice?"

### *I'm Tired, I'm Whipped*

*I'm tired*
*I'm whipped*
*too dumb to quit*
*too smart*
*to let life go by*

*I'm working hard*
*to find truth*
*in my own backyard*
*I've done everything*
*but die*

*Took the long way around*
*on a short ride to town*
*found a pass*
*where few have been*

*Gained a love*
*lost a friend*
*scraped my knees*
*learning to please*

*started out*
*with no choice*

*somewhere*
*somehow*

*found my*
*voice*

*-Nevin Compton Trammell*

4. Because inspiration sometimes comes at unexpected moments, take care to allow for down time, relaxation, "do nothing" time. You might be surprised what inspired idea comes to you when you least expect it. As a wise person said, God could not have invented a Stradivarius violin without an Antonio Stradivarius.

5. Rachel Carson's original work, *Help Your Child to Wonder* (1956) has been re-edited with stunning photographs and published under the title, The Sense of Wonder. It is a perfect book for adult and child to read together, including teacher and student.

## Group Resources

1. Think back to a high point, when you were inspired in your work, and complete this sentence: "When I am at my best with my patients/students, I am _____." Allow others in the group to comment, perhaps providing a perspective that you can't see up close.

2. Have you considered trading places briefly with another clinician or even observing each others' work? You may feel inspired from seeing new materials or watching another clinician's techniques. This relatively small effort is worth the payoff of creativity and new ideas it may engender.

3. Discuss some of the drawings in *The Dog-Exercising Machine* by Edward

deBono (who also wrote *The Six Thinking Hats*), a book of fantastic solutions by children who were challenged to invent a machine that would exercise dogs. This book oozes with inspiration, as children draw and explain the machine they have designed, unencumbered by adult notions of impossibility and impracticality.

4. Earlier in this chapter I referred to the poem, "Fire" and the meaning a teacher took from it, as quoted in *Teaching with Fire – Poetry that Sustains the Courage to Teach*. How do those in the group relate to such lines as, "Too many logs packed in too tight can douse the flames…" What "open spaces" do you need to re-kindle inspiration in your work?

# THE SIXTH DAY

# RE-CREATION OF GRATITUDE

*....Then God formed man of dust of the ground, and breathed into his nostrils the breath of life and the man became a living person.  (Gen. 2:7)*

*"Normal day, let me be aware of the treasure you are. Let
me learn from you, love you, bless you before you depart.
Let me not pass you by in quest of some rare and perfect
tomorrow. Let me hold you while I may, for it may not always be so. One day I shall dig my nails into the earth, or
bury my face in the pillow, or stretch myself taut, or raise
my hands to the sky and want, more than all the world,
your return."*          -Mary Jean Irion

## Overwhelming Gratitude

*Well, it's Saturday, the sixth day of Creation, the beginning of the
week-end, a welcome day, a time to greet with joy. And in the cycle
of the week, this is the moment I come face to face with what the
biblical writers consider the ending achievement of the Creation's
Order of Days, Mankind and the human family. I have to admire
the literary talent of the ancient Biblical writers. There are two different Hebrew versions of the creation of Man, and both of them
display the majestic uniqueness of human beings compared to everything else in Creation. I know there are many who see this in a
different light, viewing Man as only one ingredient of the Creation
Process; unique, yes, but no more so than a daisy or that mourning
dove I wrote of earlier. Just as the daisy and the mourning dove
and all the rest of created living things are changing, still under the
influence of God's initial creative thrust, so is the human family.*

*The Bible clearly sees the human family as the ultimate act of God's
love for a world, which tells this story from Genesis to Revelation.
The Psalmist rhapsodized over God's ultimate creature:*

*....what is man that thou art mindful of him and the son of man
that thou dost care for him? Yet thou hast made him little less than
God and does drown him with glory and honor. Ps. 8:5*

IN RECOGNIZING GOD'S CREATION OF HUMANKIND AS HIS MOST MAGNIFICENT
accomplishment, I profoundly sense my obligation to live in thankfulness. After
all, humans have been blessed with the unique ability to feel and express gratitude. So, on this sixth day of Re-Creation, I write about gratitude and re-creating
a sense of appreciation, of thankfulness in my life, both professionally and personally. It is an important topic for me to cover, because I have been guilty at times of
viewing situations without the "attitude of gratitude" that I have tried so hard to
develop in my children. There's nothing like our children to make us want to crawl

into a hole in the ground, when they show appreciation for their parents in a way we probably don't deserve. When my son, Luke, spoke at church about why he was volunteering to spend a week repairing homes in rural Kentucky as part of a team for the Appalachian Service Project, he told the congregation, "It's simple. My parents have always instilled in us that we have been given so much, we are obligated to take on an attitude of gratitude." How satisfying to know that he is learning this in his own life.

> *I read a quote in my devotional book today by Karl Barth: "Joy is the simplest form of gratitude." How true this rings for me! Yet, I'm not always sure exactly how to make it a reality. But even if I don't know how to practice gratitude perfectly, this quote is the reminder I need that God must take great pleasure when I feel and express joy in my life. Joy is the outward expression of the inward sensation of thankfulness.*

## Saturday's Child

I TAKE SPECIAL JOY IN WRITING THESE THOUGHTS TODAY BECAUSE I AM TRULY a Saturday child. In fact I was born on a Tuesday, but I am Saturday's child as described in the Mother Goose rhyme, "Monday's child is fair of face, Tuesday's child is full of grace, Wednesday's child….." Saturday's child in this rhyme is a child "who works hard for a living." Sometimes I wish I were Sunday's child who is "fair and wise and good and gay." I know myself well enough to say I certainly am not always wise or fair. I can be good, but I can be bad too; and I am often melancholy rather than filled with Robert Louis Stevenson's "gaiety of mind." So as a person who works for a living - as a partner of course with my husband in family economics - I sometimes allow Saturday to become the sixth day of my work week. Alas! I know as well as anyone that even a five-day work week can make Jill a dull girl. And when Saturday becomes a work day rather than a day of play, merriment and the frolicking memories of childhood extravagance, we deny with what wisdom the Creator has ordained the progression of days of the week.

Saturday stands as a gate leading from the five days of the work week and our presentation on Sunday for spiritual inspection. In times past our culture seems to have understood this better than today. Historically Saturday was a true family day, a time for cultivating our spirit at the library or maybe at a movie matinee or browsing through the riches in "the little shop around the corner." It was a time for writing letters to loved ones or taking a walk (not a drive!) over to Aunt Lucy's or baking cookies for the Dillon family who were mourning a death in the family. These activities are nothing less than spiritual disciplines because they cultivate the inner spirit of generosity. They allow us to express caring that our confining work week does not normally allow.

The divine creative process never ends. When paying the mortgage, the loan on our car, supplying our children with the latest gadgets, or keeping up with the Somebody Elses becomes the center of all our labor, we are grossly handicapped in living the Saturdays of re-creative gaiety and renewal. If you will, at this very moment, look out a window where you are. You might see trees reaching skyward as you and I do for spiritual renewal. Or perhaps you can watch a drooping sunflower, having closed down for the night, turn completely upward for the energy of the new day's sun. Maybe you can see that a bird's face is always closer to heaven than its feet. Saturday is a gift to us for watching trees reach and sunflowers turn and birds eye their pie in the sky.

Let Saturday be what Saturday was meant to be, a day to shake off the work week in order to come before the Lord on the Sabbath as one who has tasted the wine of life. Saturday is for play, for gaiety of the mind, for exploring all that God has laid out for us in this exorbitant Feast. St. Augustine wrote that God is always trying to give good things to us but our hands are too full to receive them.

When I was in the early years of Elementary School, we lived very near the western bank of the Missouri River as it flows past Omaha and Bellevue. Looking across the river to the east we could see the high rising bluffs of Iowa. On Saturdays when the weather was nice my father and some of my sisters and brother would take a tent and a lunch, go across the river and up onto the high bluffs. We'd pitch the tent, take walks along the steep bluffs, and eventually get back into the tent for our lunch. We would lie in the tent on sleeping bags and tell stories and while away a nice Saturday afternoon. Oh, the view from those bluffs! In his poem "Foreign Lands" Robert Louis Stevenson writes about the view from the upper branches of the cherry tree, "And looked abroad on foreign lands." Just as standing on high bluffs or being perched atop a cherry tree is like looking upon a foreign land, so it seems the higher we go in our understanding of God's creative purpose, the clearer our view becomes of our own spiritual self, our unlimited capacities for becoming a whole person. I know now that on those Saturday afternoons up on the Iowa bluffs with my father and my siblings I was given a taste of the kind of Saturday God had in mind when he created this human family. Saturday can become again what God created if we just let go, even for an afternoon, our money making and busy-beeing and let God replenish our spirits so that we have a clearer view of this unbelievably rich life God has given us. High on an Iowa bluff a person practically can see infinity.

# Gratitude and the Now

I SUSPECT THAT GRATITUDE IS ALMOST INSEPARABLE FROM THE NOTION OF THE Present, the Now, living this moment fully, under whatever circumstances we've been dealt. I've quoted Robert Louis Stevenson quite a lot in this book because his poetry represents a slice of my childhood, a time of innocence when my father, who has hundreds of poems memorized would tuck us in at night and recite one of them.   Some of Stevenson's poems are very well-known such as, "The Swing" and "The Land of Counterpane." But the one I most remember my dad reciting, when he tucked us in at night, is a wistful poem, "The Lamplighter" about a child watching dusk fall through his London window as Mr. Leary lights the gas street lamps one by one. The child expresses gratitude at having a streetlight so close to their home, for safety and illumination at night. But then - and we assume this is Stevenson himself speaking, a sickly child whose over-protective parents required him to stay in bed most of his childhood – the child asks for a tiny gesture of human communication:  "For we are very lucky with a lamp before our door; And Leary stops to light it as he lights so many more. But, oh before you hurry by, with ladder and with light; O, Leary, see a little child, and nod to him tonight." When the poem is read aloud, as I feel most poems are best expressed, we hear the child's gratitude, followed by a longing for something more. Is there any one of us who can't relate to that?

In addition to poetry, of course, Robert Louis Stevenson was a prolific writer of prose, novels, and a beautiful collection of prayers. Several summers ago, our family went to Scotland and while in Edinburgh found the Robert Louis Stevenson museum, after huffing and puffing our way up one of the winding, hilly passages that breaks off of Prince's Street. I felt a connection with a long-lost relative, a sort of pilgrimage to a holy place, considering my Scottish McConkey heritage, and the fact that my oldest son is named Patrick Campbell, both family names. Anyway, at this rather small but fascinating museum, I read something Stevenson had written, and copied it down on a scrap of paper that I still have:

> "The best things are nearest:  breath in your nostrils, light
> in your eyes, flowers at your feet, duties at your hand, the
> path of God just before you. Then do not grasp at the stars,
> but do life's plain, common work as it comes, certain that
> daily duties and daily bread are the sweetest things in life."
> Dear Lord, help me remember that sweetness when the
> "daily duties" seem monotonous and stale.
>  -Robert Louis Stevenson

# Gratitude as a Choice

I'VE BEEN READING ON THIS SUBJECT A THOUGHT-PROVOKING BOOK, *THE POWER of Appreciation* by van Kaam and Muto. One of the many things I am grateful for is the presence of those in the broader Indianapolis community who, in the words of Parker Palmer, desire congruence between "soul and role" (*Courage to Teach Guide*, p. 22). Ron Mead, System Vice President and Chief Mission Officer for St. Vincent Health in Indianapolis generously has shared many resources with me, including the writings of van Kaam and Muto. Their work focuses on formative spirituality, the details of which I am still learning about. But the title of the book, even if I don't understand all the theological intricacies, is crystal clear. Van Kaam lived in Holland during the Nazi siege of WW II when the Germans cut that country off from all supplies, food and medical care. He observed the difference in the coping strategies of those who remained hopeful, even appreciative of each day, and those who experienced depreciation (I'll explain their special meaning of this word in a moment.) These authors share their conviction that, "Appreciation is the single most important disposition to be cultivated in our life and world today." They note that this mindset of appreciation, our attitude of gratitude if you will, begins with the belief that people are born with the capacity to select the components of their lives that will give them the most joy, peace, dynamism and delight. This is not a "pleasure-of-the-moment" philosophy, but rather a life view to make sense out of the moments that encompass our human existence and to find lasting meaning in life.

But of course, life is lived moment by moment, and I do wrestle with the conflict between the big picture (All will be well when we understand the full meaning of existence) and the daily challenges and sorrows that assault us in real life. A poem by Vaclav Havel, "It Is I Who Must Begin," expresses some of this dissonance for me and was quoted often in the days just after 9/11. The poet addresses only himself in the poem, just as we are the only ones who can truly speak to ourselves in deciding whether we live a life of appreciation or depreciation.

Van Kaam and Muto point out that when we make a decision to live in gratitude, we tend to develop attitudes and acts that enable us to see the "more than" in the midst of a crisis, rather than the "less than"(p. 23). I like these words very much. For me, they are a more fitting description of the "glass half full/half empty" metaphor. The authors note, "From the first moment we acknowledge that depreciation is disrupting the way we want to feel, we deflate its dark power." I have started practicing these authors' suggestion of being aware of "JNIs" or "Just Noticeable Improvements" in situations, in other people or in myself and my actions toward others. One by one, the JNIs accumulate until they amount to quite a substantial improvement, and every once in a while, a sense of gratitude will come over me, as if I have received a gift from God.

*Gift*

> A day so happy,
> Fog lifted early, I worked in the garden
> Hummingbirds* were stopping over honeysuckle
> flowers.
> There was no thing on earth I wanted to possess.
> I knew no one worth my envying him.
> Whatever evil I had suffered, I forgot.
> To think that once I was the same man did not
> embarrass me.
> In my body I felt no pain.
> When straightening up, I saw the blue sea and
> sails.
>                    -Czeslaw Milosz

## More Than/Less Than

YES, THE DAY THE POET DESCRIBES IS A GIFT, AND I HAVE HAD DAYS THAT could only be described as such. "The soul should always stand ajar, ready to welcome the ecstatic experience," Emily Dickinson wrote. But, as with each day of this week of re-Creation, there is the cycle of positive and negative feelings, ups and downs, a day of ecstasy followed by what seems to be a day of losses. I have been struggling lately with the "more than/less than" paradox of watching as, one by one, my three boys are heading off to college. Intellectually, I know I should see this as a "more than," as a gift, that they are independent, maturing, able to thrive in a new, challenging environment. But, in the weeks after my first son left for college, I didn't feel that way – I felt a "less than," a sense of loss. I wrote to Dad about this. In the mail came a manila envelope with a huge, dried leaf, as big as the envelope, and a poem Dad had written:

> The autumn leaves, sere, golden brown
> In crisp-ed breeze, came tumbling down.
> They never felt parental yoke,
> Every tie they cruelly broke,
>          Yet parents wept.

> To see one's child release its ties
> Creates a world of moans and sighs.
> And through the treetops, elm and pine,
> Parental grasp now left behind,
>          I hear the voice, "The child is free."

**\*More on my quest for the elusive hummingbird on the Seventh Day**

*Still through the leaves, and in the air,*
*I hear parentals' voice so fair*
*"However far you choose to stray,*
*Whatever happens on your way,*
*"You're still my child."*

Oh, the gratitude I felt! To be reminded that I hadn't lost my son, that he was "still my child", and also the gratitude that God has given me a father who could console me, who could make me see the "more than" rather than "less than" in a situation by composing a poem and mailing me a golden brown leaf.

Gratitude, as we've said, includes a commitment to live in the now, in the present, with whatever the day brings. Easier said than done, I know. But, the simple, unchangeable fact is: It is today in which I live! How often do I try to deny this day to let my mind wonder to past regrets or insults, or to fast-forward to worry about the future. I've referred already on these pages to Eckart Tolle's book, *The Power of Now.* How valuable this and other resources were in helping me live just one day at a time after my nephew, Casey, suffered a life-threatening head injury. And, when the thought of losing someone so dear to me was staring me down, with one crisis after another to be handled, how I wished longingly for "the treasure of the ordinary day," mentioned in the quote at the beginning of this chapter. It was during this dark time that I first became acquainted with O'Donohue's writings, especially a quote so applicable to what I was experiencing. "The things we never notice like health, friends and love, emerge from their subdued presence and stand out in their true radiance as gifts we could never have earned or achieved" (pg.22).

## The Power of Gratitude in Parents

*As I write in my journal of the capacity to feel gratitude, what comes to mind immediately are the parents of children with whom I work. These mothers and fathers have lived through the traumatic, sometimes devastating experience of being told their child has a disability, a genetic disorder, a special condition. Each parent responds to this in his or her own way and time, and we clinicians know the range of emotion and reactions that different families express. But, I remain astounded at the coping power of so many of the parents I see. They cry, they grieve, they mourn, sometimes they can't imagine happiness ever touching their lives again. Other parents who have previously gone through this experience can be invaluable at this point. As one mother of an older deaf child told the parents of a newly-diagnosed deaf baby, "Believe it or not, you will laugh again!" In their own time and at their own pace, parents start to heal and slowly to regain a sense of normalcy. But what astounds me is how many parents go beyond just coping or a*

*return to normalcy. Many parents with whom I've worked eventually, with the passing of time, feel an enhanced sense of gratitude, appreciation, thankfulness. Some say they appreciate their children and life in general, in a more intense way, that they are actually MORE grateful than they were before their child's diagnosis. What process of the human mind and heart makes this possible? I can't begin to know, but it happens often, and many of my colleagues have observed and spoken of it. Its presence can truly be one of the Thin Places of our work in this profession.*

## The Risk of Idealism in the Tragic Gap

AS I FOCUS ON GRATITUDE AND THE WAY FAMILIES OVERCOME OBSTACLES, I am reminded again of the tragic gap – this time a gap in which parents try to hold the tensions between what could be and what is. In this case, the temptation, the "feel-good" approach, is to embrace what Parker Palmer calls "a dreamy idealism, living a life of cheerful irresponsibility that floats above the fray." As clinicians, we sometimes have been guilty of using a "minimize the problem" approach with parents, fearing that our more honest words will produce an emotional response that we are unprepared to handle. I could look at the acceptance of parents of my special-needs patients and decide this is just a sweet, wonderful world with nothing but happy endings. To do so would do a disservice to the "tragic gap" in which these families themselves stand, and the tensions they balance on an almost daily basis.

With permission, I quote from the writings of a mother of one of my 4-year old patients: "I am discovering that this particular journey with hearing loss, like the rest of my life, is always evolving. As I receive new information I will ask God to help me understand it. I realize that this particular journey with Patrick has the potential to make my family and each individual stronger and more spiritual than if Patrick did not have this condition. I understand now that Patrick is a gift and I continually ask God for the ability to recognize this gift as it presents itself as I know it will take on many forms and they won't always be easy and will, sometimes, even be painful."

Parents also speak about the positive effects on other siblings of having a special-needs child in the family. Of course this perspective does not come immediately, but as with many forms of Gratitude, is revealed over time. Patrick's mother continues: "The two real 'victories' that stand out in my mind, and I know my husband's as well, came as a surprise to me. The first one was when we began to notice that Patrick was exhibiting a real personality. We thought that this would be compromised because he was deaf so we were literally dumb-founded as we watched him evolve. My gosh, was he something else to watch! The second, and equally as amazing to us, was the relationship he was developing with his two older brothers. We clearly didn't see this coming and it was intoxicating. I think since we had no idea what to expect we were always taken aback when something, like seeing him with his brothers, unveiled itself. Watching my other two sons with Patrick has given me the ability to see Patrick as himself and not my deaf son. They simply look at him as their sometimes annoying little brother who often makes them laugh hysterically."

My Nebraska country-western music roots keep me grounded sometimes, especially when they tell compelling stories, as in Tim McGraw's *Live Like You Were Dying*. He sings from the perspective of his father who has been given news of incurable cancer. The father tells his son how he reacted after the diagnosis:

> " I loved deeper
> And I spoke sweeter
> And I gave forgiveness I'd been denying.
> And," he said, "Someday I hope you get the chance
> To live like you were dying."

## Life's a Twinkling

PART OF GRATITUDE, TRUE GRATITUDE, IS KNOWING WE DON'T HAVE FOREVER on this planet. We have only the briefest of time, yet how sweet it can be. Carrie Newcomer sings in *The Gathering of Spirits* that, "…..life's a twinkling that's for certain, but it's such a fine thing." Clay and I attended a spirituality workshop at Duke Divinity School about three years ago, and were asked as part of our registration forms to give a title for an autobiography we might write about our life. For mine I chose those lines of Carrie's: "Life's a Twinkling, But Such a Fine Thing."

One of my favorite reminders that "life's a twinkling" is another of the notes that I've already mentioned my dad leaves for his children. This particular note is water-spotted and the edges are curling because it is held by a magnet to my bathroom medicine cabinet and I see it several times each day. It's just a list of suggestions for me that I found after Dad left here several years ago, after a visit. Some are expressions of gratitude, but lest you think my father, the Methodist pastor, is pious and reverent at all times, read on:

> Be happy
> Love someone who is unlovable
> Do one ridiculous thing each day
> Learn the third verse of "The Star Spangled Banner"
> Write a poem
> Jump over something
> Have cereal and toast for supper
> Read a history of the Boer War

*Hold a fish worm in your hand*
*Have a pair of shoes re-soled*
*Taste salt*
*Write God*
*Draw six pictures of a cow*
*List the names of five people you've hated in pencil, then erase*
*Say a bad word*
*Save one toenail clipping*
*Read Psalm 50 just before the sermon*
*Kick yourself*
*Practice laughing before a mirror*
*Sleep on the floor once*
*Listen to a mourning dove*
*Hold your breath as long as you can while saying the names of*
*people you love*

## Reminders of Gratitude

T HAT WAS A GREAT REMINDER FROM DAD, PART SERIOUS, PART SILLY, PART spiritual. One thing I've learned the hard way about Gratitude is that I have to keep reminding myself over and over and over again to be thankful. I think that's because every single day, we are assailed with incidents and messages, overt or subtle that undermine our sense of Thankfulness. Hard as I try, the feeling doesn't stay unless I work at it, it must be replenished. That's why I try to surround myself and have shared in the Resources section in each chapter, reminders and examples and urgings to keep Gratitude in the forefront. Sometimes, if I'm in a "less than" mind-set and searching for a blessing for which to be thankful, I go to an anonymous quote that I consider my backup prayer: "We give thanks for unknown blessings already on their way." That just about covers it.

*I think of Saturday as Peace Day. When Isaiah writes of a time to come when, "The wolf will dwell with the lamb, and the leopard lies down with the kid, and the calf and the young lion and the yearling together....(Is. 11:6) He must surely have been thinking of Saturday, this sixth day of Creation. I don't think Isaiah had in mind any quick fix for war and marital discord and parent-child conflicts. I think he had in mind the re-ordering of our separate lives. "Give peace a chance" is not only an anti-war slogan, it is a fulfillment of God's gift of Saturday wherein we make our peace, create our peace, live our peace and express our gratitude for that peace. "My peace I give unto you" said Jesus (John 14:27) "but not as the world gives." Peace in our spirits can mend broken hearts and break down walls of separation. How slowly I have learned to use God's gift of Saturday in this way.*

# Gratitude and Prayer

THE MOTHER OF MY TEN-YEAR OLD STUDENT, COLLEEN, SHARED HER INSIGHTS about prayer and how her family prayed after their daughter's diagnosis of deafness:

> "[Other relatives] seemed to be devoting their energies toward praying for a miraculous cure--some answer that would restore Colleen's hearing. I remember feeling that God had sent me this beautiful daughter--nothing had changed except that she was going to need me more than ever. I never lost hope that she would be able to do or accomplish whatever she wanted. My only goal was to instill a strong sense of self-esteem and self-confidence in her, and to never let her feel there was something "wrong" with her. Rather than pray for miracles, I prayed for guidance in making the best decisions for Colleen, and for patience with the frustrating task of functioning as her primary communication teacher. Now, many years later, I look back and think that the most critical thing I remember reading, however, was a passage that gently reminded me that the most important gift I could give my child was not the gift of communication; rather, it was the gift of a positive self-image. I can gratefully and wholeheartedly report that in this, I have been extremely successful!"

I doubt many would disagree with that assessment after looking at Colleen's recent journal entry. The teacher asked the children to describe one thing they would change about themselves. Colleen wrote, "If I could change one thing I would not change anything. I like myself exactly how I am. I don't really worry about myself. I just don't see why other people want to change who they are. That's why I don't want to change anything about myself." This from a child with profound hearing loss and two cochlear implants! Other words of gratitude come from another mother of a seven-year old patient with a hearing loss that may be progressive over time:

> "When I stop to think about his hearing loss I definitely get teary-eyed. But not in a pathetic way because I know I am very blessed with Louis. God must know that together our family can handle this disability, especially Louis, who does so with ease and grace. Personally, I feel very connected to a greater force when I'm out in nature – somewhere grand like the mountains or ocean. An outside jog or in church is where I feel most peaceful."

One of the most sensitive expressions of parental gratitude and acceptance of who we are was given by the mother of a six year old boy whom I evaluated for learning disabilities. The little boy was trying to do his homework one night, clenched his fists with frustration and cried, "I wish God had given me a different brain!"

Though his mother ached inside hearing these words, she comforted her son and said, reassuringly, "If we changed the brain God gave you, I know your school work might be easier. But, think of all the other things about you that you do so well that would also change. Would not want to change the way your brain helps you draw such beautiful pictures of rainbows, or change your brain's witty side that lets you say such funny things that make everyone happy when they laugh at your jokes? I think I like your brain just the way it is." Thanks to a mother who could see the gratitude of the whole (the "more than" rather than "less than") this young boy is moving ahead slowly but surely in his academic progress, his confidence increased by realizing that, as with all of us, our brains are good at some things and not good at others. We are loved by God, our parents, our teachers and health-care providers, for exactly who we are. I remain in awe of parents who conjure up these responses to the tough questions youngsters pose, supporting their special-needs children with acceptance and thankfulness for their uniqueness.

> *Isn't this what the Bible means when it says we are created in the image of the Creator? Are any of us less God-like because we act or live God-less? No, of course not! Whether we come short of the Divine Image or not we are still created in the Divine Image. Some day I hope to know enough about theology to explain that fully to my little student if he doesn't already know it already.*

## Prayer and Our Work with Children and Families

THERE HAS BEEN MUCH DISCUSSION ABOUT THE USE OF PRAYER AS A practice by health-care workers or others caring for special-needs children. As with all matters of faith, feelings run strong on both sides of this issue. In an article in *Research News and Opportunities in Science and Theology* (October, 2003; Vol 4, No. 3) various experts weighed in on this debate with thoughtful comments pro and con. Both Christina Puchalski, director of The George Washington Institute for Spirituality and Health and Dr. Harold Koenig from Duke University's Center for the Study of Religion/Spirituality and Health felt that talking to patients or the families of patients about their faith was absolutely appropriate if the family identified faith and spirituality as part of their support system - just as a physician would ask about other self-reported supportive practices such as exercise, therapeutic massage, or social interactions with friends. Dr. Koening did draw the line on unsolicited prayer with patients. When asked if he would ever pray with a patient, he said, "Only if I had asked their permission first and only if I knew before I asked that their answer would be 'Yes'". I agree totally and know exactly what he was getting at – that health care providers should never impose religious beliefs on a patient who objected to them. But, what if we weren't sure? What if we didn't know a patient or a family well enough to predict their answer beforehand? Would we ever ask if a family wanted us to pray with them? I think my answer has always been no, and still would be, had I not had a personal experience that demands my attention. After my college-aged nephew, Casey, had made an initial recovery from his serious head injury, he required several surgeries and procedures. My sister told me that before and after these procedures, she would always ask Casey, a young adult, if he would like her to say a prayer. His answer was always 'no.' "So, I respected that," Anne said, "and never prayed in front of him."

Then an incident landed them in the Emergency Room of the hospital, where they had been several times in the past few months. A different ER doctor treated Casey then told him he was free to leave. And he added, "Casey, would it be helpful to you if we said a prayer together?" Anne reports, "I held my breath, embarrassed, because I knew Casey would decline the offer. But, to my amazement, Casey replied, 'Yes, I'd like that'. And the doctor said a short prayer, a prayer of gratitude, thanking God for the healing that God had already made possible for my son." Casey's spirits lifted, and he left the ER, according to his mother, with a sense of hopefulness. Was this any different from a doctor asking "Casey, would it be helpful if I gave you some cold compresses for your head? Or, "Casey, would it be helpful if you spoke to a psychologist about your accident?" I believe that, within reason what patients view as contributing to their own wellness or healing should be offered to them, along with what expert health care providers know to be proven treatments and standards of care. If this ER doctor had asked Casey's mother beforehand, "Do you think he would want me to say a prayer with him?" there is no question that the answer would have been "no." Yet predicting how you may react in a given situation is impossible, not until you're in it, you're deep in it, and during Casey's fifth ER visit, he felt the desire to accept a prayer on his behalf.

## When Health Care and Faith Intersect

BEING WITH A FAMILY WHO HAS SENT THEIR CHILD INTO SURGERY IS ONE OF the situations clinicians have cited where they are most likely to be asked to pray with parents. My former colleague, Allyson who is Jewish, told me she sat with the mother of her patient as the child was undergoing cochlear implant surgery. The mother, a Christian, asked Allyson to pray with her, for her child's safety and for the surgeon that he might use good judgment during the procedure. Allyson said, "It felt perfectly natural that I, an observant Jew and this mother a Christian, would be saying a prayer together. After all, we were praying to the same God." Another colleague, Teri, who is Lutheran shared stories of the memorable times she was asked by parents to pray for their deaf children. On two different occasions, Muslim mothers made that request of her. Teri recalls feeling that the mothers respected her role as an educator but also felt a unity with her because she was a believer. One woman's family had made an offering at a special site to pray for the healing of their child's deafness, and that included preparation of lamb. Their tradition was to distribute the meat from the offering to people whom they felt shared in the process of prayer and spiritual support for their child, and this family gave some of the meat to Teri. Like Allyson, Teri said that she felt a sense of oneness, praying and sharing traditions with women of very different faiths.

I have spoken to many colleagues about this issue and am impressed by how respectful they strive to be when patient care and spirituality intersect. Joseph Roberson, M.D. is an internationally-known otologist in Palo Alto, and CEO of the California Ear Institute. Dr. Roberson has shared with me how fundamental his Christian faith is to everything he does in his life and work. It has led him to establish the Let Them Hear Foundation that sends medical teams to countries such as Costa Rica, Peru, China Bulgaria, Singapore, Indonesia, and Nepal to fund and perform cochlear implant surgeries and to provide training to doctors in those countries so that the work may continue in those places. But, Dr. Roberson emphasized that it is of the utmost priority that he and his staff treat every patient they encounter, regardless of religious affiliation, or in some cases lack thereof, with exactly the same standard of care. As suggested by the experts in the article from Research *News and Opportunities in Science and Theology* mentioned earlier, Joe first asks people what might be of value to them, particularly before surgery. He may offer, "I see you are nervous. What do you need? Medication, more time, prayer, more information?" If the patients include prayer in their response, he replies, "Do you want me to pray alone for you or do you want to pray together?" At each step, he goes "only as far as the patient wants to go." He noted that children in his practice sometimes ask him questions about his faith and that he and one little boy have an ongoing discussion about Jesus Christ whom Joe refers to as "my man."

That a child brings to his doctor questions of faith speaks to the trusting relationships these doctors have cultivated. Many physicians say they would not want to practice medicine without such relationships because they give deep and lasting meaning to their vocation. Richard Miyamoto, M.D., my friend and colleague of many years here in Indianapolis, is a world-renowned otologist and Chairman of the ENT department at the Indiana University School of Medicine. With permission, I share this story of a letter he received from a young child in his practice who wrote, "Dear Dr. Miyamoto: Why did God make me deaf? Does God love other kids more than me?" Rich says his response to this child was one of the hardest letters he has had to write, because he wanted to say the right thing and thought long and hard about his answer. He wrote back, saying that, although he couldn't answer the child's first question about why God had made him deaf, he could say with certainty that God loved this boy just as much as God loved all other children. He added that it was because the child had a hearing loss that Rich had been able to meet him and become friends with him and Rich considered their friendship to be a great gift. As parents, we can only hope that when our children ask such questions – questions with which most adults grapple – they will have health care providers who respond as openly and lovingly as Dr. Roberson and Dr. Miyamoto.

Occasionally I have prayed with families during therapy sessions, at their request; not often, because as I said, this still feels like very shaky ground. But, even if I do not pray aloud with most families with whom I work, I feel a prayerful connection in other ways. Frequently, in my daily prayers, I pray for the children with whom I work, and for their parents, asking God to show me the wisdom to do the right thing to help that child and his parents. My colleagues have shared many ways that they connect spiritually, in essence "praying" with the special-needs children and families with whom they work, even if they do not say a prayer out loud. Some of the ways mentioned are gentle touch, encouraging facial expressions and body language, laughter when irritation might be expected, and especially, supportive words. We might consider all of those forms of prayer. As Rumi, the 13th century Sufi poet wrote, "There are a thousand ways to kneel and kiss the ground."

## Connection Prayers

I HAVE WRITTEN THAT I PRAY FOR MY PATIENTS EVEN THOUGH THEY DON'T know that I do so. This reflects my larger way of looking at prayer, which includes the practice of journaling, singing hymns, reciting poetry and entering into contemplative meditation. There is another way to "kneel and kiss the ground" that I've tried. This other way fits with my thoughts of Saturday as Peace Day and as a day to express gratitude. How do we express love to those close to us? That seems like an easy answer – we express it by how we respond to them, speak to them, interact physically with them. But what about our expression of love to the many nameless people – strangers, really - with whom we cross paths every day? The faces of people I pass, but do not know or speak to, day after day at a large medical center. I think of this especially when I travel. As I walk through airports and pass hundreds of people going the opposite direction on the moving walkways, we are so disconnected. We actually avoid eye contact, as if all the others around us are nonexistent.

Years ago, I saw a televised interview with Richard Gere in which he talked about his Buddhist faith. Gere described the Buddhist practice of connecting with strangers by making eye contact and saying silently to them, "I love you and I wish you peace" or some other affirmation. I was intrigued by this, not just because Richard Gere suggested it (okay, yes, partly because Richard Gere suggested it) but also because it seemed to be a way to connect with others, even those outside our small sphere of contact. It reminded me of the song, "Let there be peace on earth, and let it begin with me" and of the prayer of St. Francis of Assisi, "Make me an instrument of your peace." Another connection prayer I've used is, "I thank God for you" as an expression of gratitude for each created human soul. I began trying this connecting practice when I traveled. I would recommend you try it too. As a stranger comes toward me, I intentionally make eye contact with him or her. I try to maintain eye contact long enough that our eyes actually meet each other and I can say to myself, and lift up to God, "I love you and I wish you peace." I smile at the other person. The reaction of people surprised me and would probably surprise you. I expected most people to look away immediately and avoid direct eye contact – something that might be perceived as invasive or threatening. And, in fact, there are a small number of people who do react this way. But, the majority of people have quite a different reaction that goes something like this: People notice my direct gaze and quickly look away. Then they look back again. Once our eyes actually meet, I begin my connection prayer and people overwhelmingly tend to keep looking and to smile or to just look. In any case, their look is not threatening or hostile, as I had expected. Rather, they almost seem relieved, just as I feel, to connect with someone in the impersonal and cold atmosphere of an airport. Do they know I am praying for them? That's doubtful. Does my prayer help them? Perhaps. Does my prayer help me? Absolutely.

## Ways to Give Thanks in Prayer

I PONDER AGAIN HOW IMPORTANT PRAYER IS TO MY DAILY LIFE. THEOLOGIANS and writers have offered differing views on prayer. Søren Kierkegaard said, "A man prayed and at first he thought that prayer was talking. But he became more and more quiet until in the end he realized that prayer is listening." I loved reading Anne Sexton in "Welcome Morning": "So while I think of it, let me paint a thank you on my palm for this God, this laughter of the morning, lest it go unspoken. The joy that isn't shared, I've heard, dies young." The 14th century German mystic, Meister Eckhart said, "If the only prayer we say in our life is 'thank you', that is probably enough." The exquisitely simple prayer of Dag Hammarskjold was: "Night is drawing nigh –For all that has been – Thanks! To all that shall be – Yes!"

## Give One Thing More

*As I come to the end of these six days of Creation and six days of writing my response to it, I look back on the mind-boggling story the Bible has told in these opening pages of Genesis. No Pulitzer prizes for these biblical writers but words that endure throughout time. At the close of this Saturday, I look back in my journal with awe and wonder and gratitude above all.*

*I have walked through my garden on this Saturday afternoon, and my heart fills up with all that has come together on this last day of Creation. I can't help but sing again one of the greatest hymns I know: I Sing the Almighty Power of God, this time its second stanza:*

*I sing the goodness of the Lord, who filled the earth with food,*
*Who formed the creatures through the Word,*
*and then pronounced them good.*
*Lord, how they wonders are displayed, where'er I turn my eye,*
*If I survey the ground I tread, or gaze upon the sky.*

*I do gaze up and then kneel and (symbolically) kiss the ground on this sixth day of Creation, this day in which I celebrate the human capacity for Gratitude, praying the prayer of George Herbert (1593-1632):*

> *"Thou who hast given so much to me*
> *Give one thing more:*
> *A grateful heart.*
> *For Christ's sake,   Amen."*

*I close my journal with, "And there was morning and there was evening, the sixth day."*

# Resources for Re-Creation of Gratitude:

## Individual Resources:

1. Think about making a Gratitude list or better yet, start a Gratitude journal. As a means of outward expression, acknowledge in writing things or people for whom you are thankful. William Arthur Ward wrote that, "Feeling gratitude and not expressing it is like wrapping a present and not giving it."

2. Start to pay attention to JNIs (Just Noticeable Improvements) in attitudes, responses, behaviors. Van Kaam and Muto claim that the more you notice JNIs, the more they occur, and as they build on one another, we are transformed to be more appreciative in all our interactions. Take note of whether you feel yourself moving toward a "more than" rather than a "less than" approach.

3. I dare you to try some flash prayers/connection prayers the next time you travel!

4. Gratitude is a choice. "Anyone who looks for the good can always find much for which to be grateful, or he can dwell on the present evil and wreck his composure." (Louise W. Eggleston). When faced with this choice, how have you responded in the past?

## Group Resources:

1. Do the words in this quote from Van Kaam and Muto match your experience?: "Feeling appreciative thoughts and living accordingly makes the difference between appraising one's life as ultimately meaningful or ultimately meaningless." (p. 11)

2. What thoughts do you have about the use of spirituality as a clinical tool for patients or families who express this as something that supports them? What about prayer? In the case of children who ask care-givers about God and spiritual issues, *Prayers for the Little Ones* by Julia Cameron are lovely, especially her "Inner Voice Prayer." There are prayers for children of many different faith traditions included in Cameron's book.

3. As we relate to one another, even those we do not know, could connection prayers be a positive force? Has anyone in the group tried this, and if so, what has been the reaction?

4. Play a recording of Norah Jones' haunting version of *American Anthem,* written by Gene Scheer and used on the PBS series, *The War.* The chorus repeats, "Let them say of me I was one who believed, in sharing the blessings I received." Whether you interpret this as a patriotic or personal message, how does it speak to how we pass along our gratitude? Do we owe something to others?

5. Dave Sindrey shared this saying below with me. Do you find in it a different perspective on gratitude for what one has accomplished?

*Success*

*To laugh often and much;*
*To win the respect of intelligent people and the*
*affection of children;*
*To earn the appreciation of honest critics and*
*endure the betrayal of false friends;*
*To appreciate beauty, to find the best in others;*
*To leave the world a bit better, whether by a*
*healthy child, a garden patch*
*Or a redeemed social condition;*
*To know even one life has breathed easier because*
*you have lived.*
*This is to have succeeded.*
               *-Bessie Stanley*

# THE SEVENTH DAY

# RE-CREATION OF FAITH

*Thus the heavens and the earth were finished,*
*and all the host of them.  And on the seventh day*
*God finished the work which he had done, and he*
*rested on the seventh day from all his work…*
*(Gen. 2:1-2)*

*Breathe through the heat of our desire*
*Thy coolness and thy balm*
*Let sense be dumb, let flesh retire,*
*Speak through the earthquake, wind and fire,*
*O still, small voice of calm.*
        *-John Greenleaf Whittier*

*"Sometimes I have loved the peacefulness of an ordinary Sunday. It is like standing in a newly planted garden after a warm rain. You can feel the silent and invisible life. All it needs from you is that you take care not to trample on it."*
*(Gilead, p. 20)*

## Sabbath Tranquility

*Sabbath Tranquility is the way Henry David Thoreau described this seventh day of creation. The serenity of sounds, quiet mood and landscape makes the Sabbath what I think it should be. I read this seventh day entry in my journal and I discover I have written, "It's as if I've come into a different world from yesterday." Of course the world itself is the same as yesterday. People, hurriedness, conflicts -even the lawn just outside this window- are the same. It isn't that the world has been transformed; it's that a change has taken place in me, in my response to the great spirit of calm that comes each week with this seventh day. It is partly a response to a laxity of commitments, to a sense of gratitude for all that's happened this past week, to the glorious story of biblical Creation and to what the day offers. Thoreau felt it, I sense it to the very depths of my spirit.*

*It is Sunday morning, early, the sun not yet up over the trees to the east. The house is quiet, my family is still asleep ("I pray thee, Lord, their souls to keep!), Spring Mill Road just a front lawn away, so usually busy with cars all the other six days is nearly empty. There are no airplanes overhead from the airport screeching and scaring the daylights out of the birds that thought this was a day of rest. Even the air has grown calm. I think those blue jays have put a damper on. I know instinctively this is the blessing God gave in Genesis 2:3, "So God blessed the seventh day and hallowed it."*

I WONDER, IS THIS SEA OF TRANQUILITY FELT IN IRAQ? IS IT POSSIBLE CHILDREN in the Darfur actually experience a calming of the waters of hunger and violence? Across this city are grieving families who have lost loved ones during the night, hospitals and hospices of Indianapolis witness to the sufferings of body and spirit. Can Sabbath serenity be felt in these places where there is no privilege of reading yesterday's journal?

Yes, yes, yes! God's promise of blessing and hallowedness was never meant to be confined. This blessing is as wide as the world God set in motion. I know the witness of too many military servicemen and women from the Library of Congress archives to realize that God has no intention of absenting himself from our human conflicts. Read the journals of the doctors and workers with Doctors Without Borders, the International Red Cross, The Children's Fund and other agencies to know how a caring worker is binding up a child's wound, giving a cup of nourishing broth, spraying a tent against flies and mosquitoes and embracing that child with words of love and comfort bring a peace that overcomes the world of that child's pain and dismay. Hospitals, private homes and families drawn together in times of lost loved ones have the blessings of peace that are truly wondrous.

*My mind goes out this morning to all these places. There will be prayers for this created world in our church this morning, and I know in spite of all the sorrows and conflicts this is still the world God created, the world God so loved, that his Sabbath tranquility is as wide as the seven seas and the seven continents. "This is the day the Lord has made, let us rejoice and be glad in it." (Ps. 118:24). Truly, truly, this is my Father's world. I remember my Jewish friends have a head start on the Sabbath with their Friday night services in temple or synagogue.*

There are of course routines even on Sundays. Some people will travel to family get-togethers or a picnic in the park, children doing catch up homework, dad may be busy with his woodworking, goin' fishing, a picnic in the park, reading the Sunday paper. Overall there is a spirit of relaxation, of release, of putting life together. For many of us, attending church will be close to the top of the list as we practice our Sabbath traditions. Norman Wirzba in Living the Sabbath writes, "Sabbath celebration completes the creation of the universe......and Sabbath worship is the week's fulfillment and inspiration." I know that if I don't make room for worship on Sunday, whether in a sanctuary or elsewhere, the day just doesn't feel right, and sometimes that means my whole week doesn't quite seem right either. Wirzba writes, "When we fail to observe the Sabbath, we miss out on the opportunity to experience creation and each other as God desires it." To experience creation? Yes, creation, with the promise of the inner holiness that comes in keeping the Sabbath.

The work, stress and demands of the past week take their toll. I sometimes wonder, in human terms, if God himself might have gotten worn out with all those six days of creating things. Making a universe is no task for slackers. I wonder, after all the excitement of seeing things come into existence, if God might have wiped his celestial brow and said, "Good heavens! I've got to go take a nap!" Perhaps, symbolically, that's what he did on this seventh day, "And on the seventh day God rested from all the work he had done" (Gen. 2:2). No wonder, whew! Now *that* makes God personal to me, since I delight in taking an afternoon snooze sometimes, a skill I learned from my father, a master of the almost instant regeneration that comes from five minutes of noonday slumber.

# Creation Continues

Wirzba asserts that the key to Sabbath observance is that "we participate regularly in the delight that marked God's own response to a creation wonderfully made." This created world, this world still being created, jolts me back to reality. Still being created? O goodness, yes. Isn't God creating families this morning? Isn't he creating young people to help in re-creating the world? He's creating a new self-reliant person after a divorce, giving stability after disruption, creating a life of faith after doubt, creating peace in lives and households after conflict. This process of creation in no way came to a halt after the 6th day, it was only the beginning and what any of us feel on this day of Sabbath Tranquility is only what began on that day and is described in the very first verse of Genesis 1, "In the beginning." Having created something means there is now room for re-creating.

I think this story of Creation leads to the asking of the inevitable question, "Now what?" What does all this mean to us in the living of our lives, practicing our faith, making our work count for something, standing in the tragic gap, reaching for that which is beyond us, striving for a completeness and wholeness in ourselves? What does Creation mean in my work, in my love for children and families, in my relationships with my co-workers? How does Creation with its powers of re-Creation affect the unlimited capacity to fashion my life as a joyous, full and faithful creation of the creating God. "O my soul, what now?"

Well, perhaps nothing. I have the temptation for that. We may go on as we've done before, indifferent to anything or anyone, including God, who intrudes on our complacency. In Julia Cameron's, *Prayers from a Nonbeliever – A Story of Faith* the writer honestly expresses her fear that if God were somehow part of her life, it would mean being less and less of herself and who she is deep inside. We are given the choice. We may continue in selfishness, in domestic violence, in the unforgiving spirit, in lives devoid of joy or daring or adventure. We may never read a book, learn a foreign language, laugh with those who laugh or mourn with those who mourn. We may never lie on our back on the lawn on a summer's night and look up at Sirius with its brightness 23 times more brilliant than the sun. We may never take our daughter dancing, our son to a baseball game, our parents to a fair or see the Northern Lights. We may, of our own choice, get stuck in the third day of Creation and never experience the seventh.

I've mentioned how as a child, Robert Louis Stevenson was often confined to his bed because of his parents' belief he had all sorts of illnesses. In this confinement, Stevenson let his imagination create new worlds of kings, queens, armies, cities, gardens and fields. "Block City" begins:

> *What are you able to build with your blocks?*
> *Castles and palaces, temples and docks.*

*Rain may keep raining, and others go roam,*
*But I can be happy and building at home.*
*-Robert Louis Stevenson*

I think Stevenson grasped something I need in my life. It is the power of the creating God to enable us to build something out of what we have and who we are, to make a life, to never give up. Isn't that what Creation is about, making new worlds out of voids, establishing harmony where there was none before, putting everything in its place when the wider scheme of things seems displaced? Yes, and more than that. It is knowing who the Creator is and living a life of gladness and rejoicing. It is continuing what has begun. On the Sabbath, we look back on our week, rejoice in what we have done well, ask forgiveness for the ways we have disappointed ourselves and others, and look ahead for the cycle of Re-Creation to begin again on Monday. This is what I must do on the Sabbath as I prepare myself for my week with my patients and their families.

## Special-Needs Children and the Tragic Gap

WHAT HAPPENS TO THOSE OF US IN THIS PROFESSION OF CARING FOR children with special needs who not only sympathize with these children but who fall in love with them? Sometimes we do this at great cost to ourselves emotionally. Again and again, Parker Palmer reminds us that standing in the tragic gap is difficult, even as we strive to be the kind of professionals who are life-giving but also pragmatic. Optimistic yet realistic. In *A Hidden Wholeness* Palmer goes so far as to say, "I harbor no illusions about how hard it is to live that way." But when I look at the alternatives, this is the choice I make. This is where I want to stand, teetering, swerving, losing my balance, but trying faithfully to maintain the tension between reality and possibility.

Rachel Naomi Remen, MD, writes that as a physician, she initially strove to keep a distance with patients, sharing in neither their disappointments nor their hopes. She labels that objective and seemingly safe relationship as "standing next to life." She adds, "Often the price of such a stance is high." Every caregiver decides for herself or himself where the fine line is between authentic caring and the creation of a dependency relationship on the part of the child, parent, or patient. Clergy, physicians, counselors of any kind know the dangers. Along with many of my colleagues, I practice the art of touch, the affirmative encouragement, the light of a smile and the attitude of listening which is a form of saying, "How precious you are to me." These are forms of healing no less powerful than antibiotics or the cleansing of a wound.

# Faith in the Future (in Small Blocks)

I WONDER, WHEN READING REMEN'S STORIES, WHICH IS HARDER: THE GIVING OF part of ourselves to patients or the detachment from them? I've come to believe the answer is that, unlike the child creating a masterpiece in "Block City," I do not have to create alone. Although I do not have everything, I have enough. This Sabbath Tranquility, this seventh day of Creation is, for me, the reminder that what God began you and I might continue together. In my professional life, the skill I do not possess a colleague does and what she does not possess, another does. Parker Palmer describes this acknowledgement as central to our ability to face the present, and to be hopeful for the future. I am not alone in my quest to better the lives of special-needs children and their families. I wonder how many times I would have to say that aloud to really believe it? Like Robert Louis Stevenson and his blocks, I am building only a piece of the future, contributing a small, but significant block to the whole. My colleagues all over the world are doing the same. This is the essence of my faith and my hope in the future. It has been an oft-recurring theme of spiritual writers from many faith traditions. Reinhold Niebuhr wrote, "Nothing that is worth doing can be achieved in our lifetime; therefore we must be saved by hope." It is written in the Talmud: "Look ahead. You are not expected to complete the task. Neither are you permitted to lay it down." A prayer of the slain Salvadoran Archbishop Oscar Romero says, "We plant the seeds that one day will grow. We water seeds already planted, knowing they hold future promise. We cannot do everything. This enables us to do something and to do it very well." I remember the witness of the English reformers, Hugh Latimer and Nicholas Ridley. Accused of heresy for preaching and teaching the Gospel against the views of Queen Mary Tudor both men were burned at the stake in 1553. As they gave up their lives, Latimer said to Ridley, "Be of good cheer Master Ridley, we shall this day light such a candle in England as I hope, by God's grace, shall never be put out." And finally, there is an inscription carved on the wood mantle above the massive fireplace at Earlham College, a Quaker school established in the Indiana wilderness in 1847. The words affirm the faith held by the college founders that their early efforts would be continued by those who came after them: "They gathered sticks, and kindled a fire and left it burning."

# Vocation Keeps Calling

*On this Sabbath, I am reading in my meditation book some writings of Meister Eckart that revisit the notion of vocational commitment: "The kind of work we do does not make us holy, but we can make it holy. However "sacred" a calling may be, as it is a calling, it has no power to sanctify; but rather as we are and have the divine being within, we bless each task we do, be it eating or sleeping or watching or any other." As I grow older I find that the joy I seek in my personal and professional life is related to my vocation of car-*

*ing for special needs children and their families, and they in turn bring me great joy. So it comes full circle. I'm reminded of this circle in Rabindranath Tagore's poem: "I slept and dreamed that life was joy. I woke, and found that life was service. I meditated, and behold! I found that service was joy."*

## Faith in Everyday Life and on the Sabbath

IN THE PREFACE TO THIS BOOK, WE SAID THAT FAITH IS NOT SOME OTHER-worldly package of perfection hanging around in the sky. Faith is what happens to us in our work, in our families and in our personal lives. I have come to see Sabbath as a beckoning back to our faith. Norman Wirzba writes of "Sabbath rest." He says, "Sabbath rest is thus a call to Sabbath trust – a call to visibly demonstrate.....that we know ourselves to be upheld and maintained by the grace of God rather than the strength and craftiness of our own hands." Several examples come to mind. The first was the testing of my faith when, as I've already mentioned, my nephew, Casey was in a coma in a Nebraska hospital after a serious head injury. The first morning I awoke at my sister's house after Casey's accident, it was 5:00 a.m. and our hope was to be at the hospital by 5:30 so we could actually speak to a physician. As I sleepily brushed my teeth, a pit in my stomach in anticipation of what the day might bring, I glanced on the wall in Anne's bathroom. There was a framed Sanskrit prayer our father had given her, "Salutation to the Dawn".

> *Look to this day!*
> *For it is the very day of life.*
> *In its brief course, lie all the truths and realities of*
> *your existence*
> *The bliss of growth*
> *The glory of action*
> *The splendor of achievement,*
> *For yesterday is but a dream*
> *And tomorrow is only a vision,*
> *But today well-lived makes every yesterday*
> *A dream of happiness*
> *And tomorrow a vision of hope.*
> *Look well, therefore, to this day!*
> *Such is the salutation to the dawn.*

Initially, I could not accept this. My beloved nephew was in ICU, clinging to life, and I was expected to rejoice in this day, to see it as "the very day of life?" In the midst of the circumstances, how could Anne and I make "today well-lived?" A thousand catastrophic thoughts wanted to spiral us downward, until we re-read the prayer and made a pact. We resolved to accomplish only two things that day: to actually speak to Casey's neurologist and to look at his CAT scan to see what injury his brain had sustained. If we could achieve those by the end of the day, we thought we could set two goals for the next day, and so on. As we sat in the ICU waiting room at 5:30 a.m., the neurologist walked by and seeing us, stopped in. He took the time to explain carefully how he viewed Casey's progress up to this point, the possible complications that lay ahead, and his overall surprise that Casey was doing as well as he was. 5:45 a.m. and our first goal was accomplished! Anne asked if a radiologist could meet with us later to go over the CAT scan. "Well, it's right back here, so let's go look at it now," the neurologist said. He reviewed the scan, pointing out the skull fracture, where bleeding had occurred, and the structures that had not been damaged by the injury. We thanked him and he went on his rounds. 6:00 a.m. and our two goals for the day were accomplished! Faith, Amy, one block at a time. And, Salutation to the dawn! Anne went home to get her first real stretch of sleep in three days. Victor Hugo's prayer was perfect at that moment: "When you have laboriously accomplished your daily task, go to sleep in peace. God is awake."

## The Faith of Janusz Korczak

A SECOND EXAMPLE OF FAITH PRACTICED IN THE REALITY OF THE PRESENT is the inspiring story of Janusz Korczak. Korczak was a renowned Polish pediatrician and author of books stressing the importance of respecting and listening to children. His work became well known across Europe in the early 20th century. As a man with ideas before their time, Korczak founded a popular weekly newspaper in 1926 called *The Little Review*, produced for and by children, that was published until the outbreak of war in 1939. Although friends begged him, a Jew, to escape as the Nazis closed in on Poland, he refused to leave the orphanages he had founded for Catholic and Jewish children. In 1940, the Nazis ordered the Jewish orphanage to be moved into the Warsaw ghetto, where Korczak's task turned from health care to tending to the dying. The description of the defiant walk Korczak lead in 1942 as he and the orphans were ordered to go to the Treblinka death camp is legendary. He organized the children to march down the streets of Warsaw, hand-in-hand in lines of four, with one child carrying the orphanage flag that Korczak had designed. He and other teachers helped the children board the trains that would take them to the gas chambers. He left a final testament called *Ghetto Diary* and wrote on the last pages, "I am angry with nobody. I do not wish anybody evil. I am unable to do so. I do not know how one can do it." In Sandra Joseph's account of these events, she says Korczak behaved as the rabbis had written: "When asked 'When everyone acts inhuman, what should a man do?' their answer was 'He should act more human.'" What strength of faith, after all he had endured, enabled Korczak, and countless others for that matter, to behave with this ultimate dignity?

## Thin Places and Silver

MY THIRD EXAMPLE OF FAITH IN THE MIDST OF REALITY SPEAKS TO THE theme of Thin Places. Soon after my father's retirement from the active ministry he began participating in archeological digs, and was at a site near Cuernavaca, Mexico in December, 2002. In letters he sent to us from Cuernavaca, he described how, on the day before Christmas, one of the Mexican workers asked my father if he would like to come to his home on Christmas Eve. My father gladly said, Yes! Getting to the home, however, turned into an act of faith and determination, as Dad became more concerned about whether he was really being sent to a legitimate place. My father was driven along a paved road in a taxi, then a gravel road, then a dirt road, and finally to no road at all. The driver pointed out to my father he would need to go down a certain path to find the house. Dad walked in the darkness through heavy brush with water on both sides of the path. Should he turn back? Faith moved him forward until, after almost falling into the water he reached the house which he found was in the middle of an actual swamp. The 'house' was only a lean-to, no plumbing, one bedroom, no refrigerator, a propane, one-burner stove. This family provided my father with a Christmas Eve that even today as I re-read the letter, brings tears to my eyes. It was a joyous family of four, they provided a meal that probably cost them a month's wages, they sang songs, lit a candle and even at 3:00 the next morning my father was not ready to come back to his quarter. He writes in his letter, "I had the feeling I was almost back at the manger, so simple were the surroundings, so joyous was the spirit of the family, so overpowering was the presence of the blessed Lord." A Thin Place can surely be found in the midst of friendship as it can in caring for our patients.

On the day my father left the project to come home this man brought him a gift from him and his family, a pair of Cuernavaca silver cuff links. My father knows what those cuff links cost that family because he had seen them in the silver market. My father says there was nothing for him to do but to stand amidst Mayan ruins embracing this man with tears on both their faces. The making of friendships that surmount differences of language, economic, ethnic and cultural barriers is surely one sign of how human community is foremost among those intentions of "God the Father who so loved the world."

## Faith, the Soul and Our Role

SUNDAY IS A TIME FOR REMEMBERING OUR ORIGINS AND THE IMMORTAL SOUL God put within us at our birth. I wrote earlier in the chapter of Julia Cameron's fear that including God in her life would somehow make her less herself. After much soul-searching, she writes in one of her last letters: "Reaching toward God has made me more me and not less me. I was always afraid you [God] would erase me. Instead, you are helping me to sketch me in." Although controversy surrounds some of his work in the field of autism, Dr. Bruno Bettelheim once gave a lecture in which he said: "I was a patient in the hospital recently. Everybody looked after me asking me about something or other. The doctor took my blood pressure, nurses asked me about my temperature, a dietician asked me about my eating habits. But during all of my hospital stay nobody, not a single person, not even the chaplain, asked me about my soul."

Not many people ask each other about their souls. Somehow that's not politically correct, it's intrusive unless done with great care and sensitivity. But God asks us about this all the time and even if we back away from asking it of our friends and neighbors, our family, isn't it a part of our faith to ask it of ourselves? O my soul, why art thou disquieted within me? (Ps. 42:5). I finally found in Parker Palmer's books a description of what I have felt for a long time but not had the words to express. In *A Hidden Wholeness*, Palmer writes of "rejoining soul and role" – ensuring that the "role" I have chosen as my vocation is a reflection of my truest self, my soul. Is the person I am with my colleagues and students and the families who trust me congruent with my inner self? I've said many times in these meditations that I'm not a theologian and I don't know very well how to define soul except in two aspects: it's what makes us who we are and it is our inner voice of truth. Our soul catches up with us, yes it does! It confronts us in the midst of a failing marriage, in the disruption of our family life, in our alcoholism, our depression, in the mistakes we make in our professional life and in our personal life. As people in the serving professions, our soul shines through us and our clients sense it. Dr. Rachel Remen tells the story of a cancer survivor who spoke to a support group and shocked her when he said, "My doctor's love is as important to me as his chemotherapy, but he does not know." She writes that she had always followed the tenet that a doctor's love didn't matter; it was only his or her professional skill that healed patients. "My training had argued me out of my truth," she says. "Medicine is as close to love as it is to science, and its relationships matter even at the edge of life itself." In our Methodist church we sing the hymn, "Praise the Source of Faith and Learning" whose words by Thomas H. Troeger underscore this idea. The last stanza is:

"As two currents in a river fight each other's undertow;
Till converging they deliver one coherent steady flow,
Blend, O God, our faith and learning till they carve a single course,
Till they join as one, returning
Praise and thanks for you, their Source."

## My Garden and the Sabbath

IN THESE TIMES SOMEHOW THE TRUTH OF THE BIBLE AS REGARDS THE SABBATH comes into focus, the focus that the Sabbath was made for man and woman. It was made so that these "streams of living water" spoken of long ago by the Psalmist might flow over us with the healing power of water, cleansing, purifying, taking away. We are always in preparation for what God prepares for us. We are like coming to a feast, we sense the aromas of what is there, we hunger for it. I think, in a way, I experienced this preparatory process in my encounter with humming-birds in my back yard. I'm thinking back to the first day of Re-creation and Emily Dickinson's notion of faith as "slants of light." Lately, my slants of light have come with wings attached. These minute hummingbirds are all green and blue, amaz-ing, fascinating creatures. But one Sunday morning, a ruby-throated one appeared, brilliant and iridescent and larger than all the other hummingbirds I'd seen. And it acted differently, too. The others flit about so quickly from branch to feeder to the fountain and then into the safe cover of the thick arbor vitae where they disappear from view. But this ruby-throated one moved slower, making it easier to track. It lingered, almost as if to check the place out and I can say there was the feeling of having some sort of spiritual experience as I sat perfectly still and observed. It went to both the hummingbird feeders which Clay had filled with nectar, but didn't drink or stop there. Then it came straight toward me as I sat motionless at the table, hovered about two feet away from me, so close I could see every detail on its mag-nificent body. It stayed so long I wondered if it might land on the table or even on my shoulder as our friends' hummingbirds did in Colorado once when we visited there.

But no, after hovering, this creature flew over to a window box, checked out the red geraniums and then disappeared in a flash. I sat perfectly still, waiting, hoping he would return. But, it was not to be. Not that day, not the next or the next. My son, Campbell, became intrigued and would join me for breakfast on the patio, to catch a possible glimpse of our new visitor. I went out every morning and waited all week for the ruby-throated hummingbird. I emailed my English colleague, Dr. John Graham, and mentioned it. John and I sometimes exchange news of weather and fauna and flora in our respective homelands. He was in the south of France at the time and mentioned the birds he was watching there, swifts and swallows and a golden eagle, but nothing so exotic, he said, as a ruby-throated hummingbird!

By the end of the week, I had pretty much given up on its return. Maybe it had been lost and just stopped here along its journey home, like a weary traveler. We looked up "ruby-throated hummingbird" in our *Birds of Indiana Field Guide* and were surprised to learn that the ruby-throated version is always a male. The other hummingbirds we regularly see are probably the same species, but are females and therefore lack the brilliant-colored throat. So, where was this bird? Why had he ap-peared and then vanished?

The following Sunday morning, having pretty much given up on seeing him again, I sat on the patio and who should re-appear exactly one week later? The elusive ruby-throated hummingbird. He didn't stay as long, didn't hover near me, he just made a quick appearance and was off, as if to say, "Relax….quit your fretting…I'm still here." Great excitement! I emailed John Graham again. This time John, now back in England, reported having a Hoopoe in his valley. I abandoned the *Birds of*

*Indiana* in favor of a broader bird guide book to find out what this Hoopoe was. On my way to looking up 'Hoopoe,' I happened across the entry for hummingbirds, and glanced at the description. What it said about the ruby-throated hummingbird startled me. It read: "The male has a black throat patch [BLACK?] that looks bright ruby red, but only when reflected in sunlight."

It took a "certain slant of light" to see the ruby-throated hummingbird as ruby-throated. What would Emily Dickinson think of this? I found it amazing this denouement came about on a Sunday morning, on the Sabbath. Norman Wirzba writes that "the Sabbath asks us to notice." Well, it took a whole week for me to notice, for my senses to recognize what was in front of me. Maybe though this really isn't surprising, it often takes a long time for something to become clear to us, for us to reap what God has been preparing. This seventh day of Creation took a lot of preparation on God's part and look what happened! In Vassar Miller's "Morning Person" the poet writes, "God, best at making in the morning, tossed stars and planets, singing and dancing……..God made us in the morning too, both man and woman, leaving Adam no time for sleep…"

We may find renewal, re-creation of vocational commitment in some of the ways I've described in these chapters. Yet there is a real danger that our lives may become so over-scheduled that there is no room for Sabbath, no room for re-Creation. After all, time is a thief. It robs us of what it means to be healers if there is not space in the interior being of our lives for spiritual renewal, re-commitment to vocation and reconciliation with the Giver of that time. What is precious to me, having rested on the Sabbath, is the thought of beginning a new week on Monday with a feeling of having been made over for the umpteenth time. It is also a coming back to the One who gave me the time in the first place and calls to me to make the most out of it I can. "Be glad and rejoice forever in what the Lord will create …." (para. of Isaiah 65.18) "The Creation continues — and we get to help!" writes D. C. Toedt.

## *Sabbath and the Cycle Starts Again*

*I close my journal now with the ending of this seven-day cycle of days of Creation. I will let today be whatever God might have in store for me. I do know that these passages from Genesis have been a wonderful source of new insight and stimuli for my faith and my work.*

*I know it all begins again tomorrow, another week, another cycle, another visit from the ruby-throated hummingbird, a challenge from our cricket-in-residence, more cherries ready to pick, the possibility that Genesis 2 will lead me in new direction of insight and possibility. As Pippa said, "All's right with the world." For that part of our world that isn't right, war and conflict, violence and evil, abuse and confusion, we like Hamlet, have been called to set it right. That's why God created the world and prepares us for it by the gift of faith renewed moment by moment, day by day, week by week, throughout life. I am content with this past week, God has blessed me.*

*I write in my journal, Thus the heavens and the earth were finished and all the host of them. And there was morning and there was evening, the seventh day.*

For my colleagues, my little patients and their families and for the readers of this book, I close with this passage from Luke's gospel (12:32), a passage that my father used as the benediction of every Sabbath service he conducted in his 50 years of ministry:

> *"Fear not, little flock, for it is your Father's good pleasure to give you His kingdom."*

# RESOURCES FOR RECREATION OF FAITH

## Individual Resources

1. "The kind of work we do does not make us holy, but we can make it holy. However "sacred" a calling may be, as it is a calling, it has no power to sanctify; but rather as we are and have the divine being within, we bless each task we do, be it eating or sleeping or watching or any other." How does this ancient quote from 13th century Meister Eckhart resonate with your sense of reverence or faith in your vocation?

2. Just as the Sabbath brings our week full-circle, so the lives of special-needs children often come full-circle as well. Vassar Miller was a gifted writer and Poet Laureate of the state of Texas who lived with cerebral palsy. Her poem, "Morning Person", was quoted earlier in this chapter and is reproduced in the Group Resources section below. Miller wrote eight books of poetry, and edited *Despite This Flesh*, an anthology of poetry and stories about people with disabilities. Her collected poems were published in *If I had Wheels or Love* and her poetry was nominated for the Pulitzer Prize in 1961. Have you lifted up to parents of special-needs children the many successful adults who flourish, in spite of their disabilities? Such examples give realistic optimism to families who worry about the unknown future of their children.

3. When I pray for children and families, I use many different resources. But this Irish prayer, sent to me by my father when Campbell was born, expresses my plea that each child, each "jewel" will be held in God's keeping.

> ### Prayer for a Child
>
> God keep my jewel this day from danger
> From tinker and pooka and black-hearted stranger
> From harm of the water and hurt of the fire
> From the horns of the cows going home to the byre
> From the sight of the fairies that maybe might change her.
> From teasing the ass when he's tied to the manger
> From stones that would bruise and from thorns of the briar
> From evil red berries that waken desire
> From hunting the gander and vexing the goat
> From depths o' seawater by Danny's old boat
> From cut and from tumble --- from sickness and weeping
> May God have my jewel this day in his keeping.
> -Winifred M. Letts

4. What are the "slants of light" in your personal life or you work? Do you feel a need for a Sabbath ritual, in whatever form it might take? Can you preserve some elements of Sabbath renewal during the workweek?

# Group Resources

1. David Ford, author of *The Shape of Living*, "tames the terror of being alive," as Ernest Becker once said, by describing how overwhelming experiences in life may become meaningful and manageable. He gives new meaning to "overwhelmed," by showing that we have the potential to be sustained by the overwhelmingly abundant love of God. Are there times that you have "overwhelmed" by something good in your work that has transformed you in a positive way?

2. How do members of the group react to these comments by Dr. Rachel Remen: "My training had argued me out of my truth. Medicine is as close to love as it is to science, and its relationships matter even at the edge of life itself."

3. In his essay called, "In Return," Janusz Korczak asked incisive questions of parents: "Do you make a gift to your child of everything which you have received from your parents, or do you only lend it to him in order to take it back again, writing everything down carefully and calculating the amount of interest due? Is love a favor for which you demand remuneration?" It is not much of a stretch to substitute words regarding our professional relationships for the words he originally used, so I have taken the liberty of inserting some substitute words that I believe are also valid: "Do you make a gift to your patients of everything which you have received from your teachers, or do you only lend it to them in order to take it back again, writing everything down carefully and calculating the amount of interest due? Is caring a favor for which you demand remuneration?" How do readers respond to these pointed questions?

4. As you contemplate on Sabbath day the winding down of the week and your preparation for a new week, what thoughts come to mind? The Sabbath always reminds me of Vassar Miller's poem, "Morning Person." Throughout this book, we have described the seven days of Creation as told in Genesis by the ancient writers. Miller, depicting the same process, condenses the Creation story, weaving each element into her joyful poem, "Morning Person." Her creation story is gleeful but no less reverent than the one described by the ancient Hebrews. How does Miller's poem strike you as you live out your own daily rising and falling, creating and recreating, in the renewing flow of God's limitless regenerative power?

*Morning Person*

*God, best at making in the morning, tossed*
*stars and planets, singing and dancing, rolled*
*Saturn's rings spinning and humming, twirled the earth*
*so hard it coughed and spat the moon up, brilliant*
*bubble floating around it for good, stretched holy*
*hands till birds in nervous sparks flew forth from*
*them and beasts–lizards, big and little, apes,*
*lions, elephants, dogs and cats cavorting,*
*tumbling over themselves, dizzy with joy when*
*God made us in the morning too, both man*
*and woman, leaving Adam no time for*
*sleep so nimbly was Eve bouncing out of*
*his side till as night came everything and*
*everybody, growing tired, declined, sat*
*down in one soft descended Hallelujah.*
    *-Vassar Miller*

# ACKNOWLEDGEMENTS

We are indebted to many who have helped with this book, including numerous colleagues who generously shared their time to speak with or write to us about their vocations. These and other colleagues encouraged us along the way to take the risk of writing a book that touches on themes of personal faith. We add that we are also grateful for what we have learned from dissenting voices.

Our heartfelt thanks go to Dr. Parker Palmer for his influence on our thinking about the "tragic gap" and other ideas in the book, and for his graciousness in reading the manuscript. We appreciate the valuable input from those who read and commented on earlier versions of the book, especially Dr. Craig Dykstra. Dr. William Placher of Wabash College and Mr. Robert Meitus provided advice regarding due diligence. The bulk of that task was accomplished with enthusiasm by Mr. Al Lyons, Indiana University – Bloomington. Al taught Amy a lesson that may be the reason this book is actually in print. He said, "A book is not finished when it is done. A book is finished when you stop writing." Thanks to Al, we eventually did stop writing. Dave Sindrey, truly our partner in this endeavor, served as so much more than a publisher and has been an integral part of the shape this book has taken from the beginning. The children and parents with whom Amy works deserve our gratitude for opening their lives and hearts to us and allowing their stories to be shared. The moral support of Neelu Sondhi and Amy's Saturday morning tennis partners, Sara, Debbie, Vickie and Jan, got the book back on track more than once when it had been derailed. We are deeply appreciative for Elantu Veovode's permission to use one of her original Celtic mandalas on the book's cover and for what she has taught us about Celtic spirituality. We gratefully acknowledge Dr. John Niparko who was the first colleague to know about our plan to write a book of this nature, and who introduced Amy to the Celtic concept of Thin Places.

Our expressions of thanks to our editor, Dr. John Wimmer, are woefully inadequate to describe his extensive contributions to this book. With humor, patience, prayer and gentle nudges, he stuck with us, gave countless hours of care to the manuscript and reminded us repeatedly of Grandma Ocie's advice to, "Jist keep a'goin." To the McConkey and Robbins clans, thank you for your excitement and support of this project and your confidence that the two least technologically-capable members of the family could somehow communicate electronically, long distance, over a three-year period. Campbell, Luke and Peter Robbins, you three are the whirlwinds and the small voices that give life meaning. Finally, loving gratitude to Clay Robbins, a man among men: you exemplify integrity, forgiveness and vocational commitment.

# SUGGESTIONS FOR FURTHER READING

Numerous authors and readings are mentioned throughout this book. The following works are particularly recommended. This compilation is included for the benefit of those readers who wish to explore in more depth any of the stories and ideas included in the book.

Bob Abernethy and William Bole, *The Life of Meaning: Reflections on Faith, Doubt, and Repairing the World*, New York: Seven Stories Press (2007)

Maggie Anderson, in *Teaching with Fire – Poetry that Sustains the Courage to Teach* (Sam M. Intrator and Megan Scribner, Editors), San Francisco: Jossey-Bass (2003), page 88

Christine Barton and Amy McConkey Robbins, *TuneUps, An Integrated Approach to Music and Speech Therapy*, Valencia, CA: Advanced Bionics Corp. www.hearingjourney.com

John Baillie, *A Diary of Private Prayer*, London: Oxford University Press, (1936)

Hyler Bracey, *Managing from the Heart*, New York: Dell Publishing (1993)

Paul Brenner, M.D., *Buddha in the Waiting Room: Simple Truths about Health, Illness and Healing*, Hillsboro OR: Beyond Words Publishing, (2002)

Emily Bronte's poem, "To Imagination," originally published in *Poems by Currer, Ellis, And Acton Bell*, London: Aylott And Jones, (1846); *The Complete Poems of Emily Jane Bronte*, New York: Columbia University Press (1941, 1995)

Judy Brown, "Fire", in *Teaching with Fire – Poetry that Sustains the Courage to Teach* (Sam M. Intrator and Megan Scribner, Editors), San Francisco: Jossey-Bass (2003), page 89

Margaret E. Bruner, "The Monk and the Peasant", from *The Hill Road*, Dallas, Texas: The Kaleidograph Press, (1932), pages 109-110

Julia Cameron, *Prayers from a Nonbeliever – A Story of Faith*, New York: Jeremy P. Tarcher (2003)

Julia Cameron, *Prayers for the Little Ones*, Los Angeles: Renaissance Books (1999)

Rachel Carson, *Silent Spring*, New York: Houghton Mifflin Co., (1962, 1990)

Rachel Carson, *The Edge of the Sea*, New York: Houghton Mifflin Co., (1955, 1998)

Rachel Carson, *The Sense of Wonder*, New York: Harper and Row, (1965)

Pema Chodron, *When Things Fall Apart: Heart Advice for Difficult Times*, Boston: Shambala Classics, (1997)

Helene Cixous, in Helene Cixous: *Rootprints: Memory and Life Writing* (by Mi Calle-Gruber), London and New York: Routledge (1997)

Susan Coolidge – "New Every Morning" in *A Few More Verses*, White Fish MT: Kessinger Publishing Company (1997) - Originally published by Roberts Brothers, Boston (1889), page 15

June Cotner, *Pocket Prayers Deck: 36 Praises & Graces for All Faiths*, San Francisco: Chronicle Books (2006)

William Cowper, "Sometimes a Light Surprises," from *Olney Hymns: In Three Parts*, (by John Newton and William Cowper), "XLVIII, Joy and Peace in Believing" (1779)

e.e. cummings, "I thank you God for most this amazing..." in *E.E. Cummings: Complete Poems 1904-1962*, Liveright Publishing Corporation (1994)

Edward de Bono, *Six Thinking Hats*, New York: Little, Brown and Company (1985)

Edward de Bono, *The Dog-Exercising Machine*, London: Jonathan Cape Children's Books (October 29, 1970)

Emily Dickinson "The soul should always stand ajar", *The Complete Poems of Emily Dickinson*, New York: Little, Brown and Company (1924, 1960), #1055, (C. 1865)

Emily Dickinson "There's a certain slant of light", *The Complete Poems of Emily Dickinson*, New York: Little, Brown and Company (1924, 1960), #82

Lloyd C. Douglas, *Disputed Passage*, New York: P. F. Collier & Son Corporation (1939)

Craig Dykstra, "Pastoral and Ecclesial Imagination." In Dorothy C. Bass and Craig Dykstra (Eds.), *For Life Abundant: Practical Theology, Theological Education and Christian Ministry*. Grand Rapids: Eerdmans Publishing Co. (2008) page 55.

Meister Eckhart (c.1260 - c.1327), *Meister Eckhart: A Modern Translation*, New York: Harper & Row (1941)

Carolyne Edwards, "Reflections on Counseling" in the newsletter *Loud & Clear!*, issue 2 (2003), available on-line at http://www.bionicear.com/userfiles/File/Issue2-2003.pdf

Suzette Haden Elgin, *How to Disagree Without Being Disagreeable*, New York: John Wiley & Sons, Inc.

Robert Frost, "Unharvested", *A Further Range*, New York: Henry Holt and Company (1936), page 62

Fred Pratt Green, "For the Fruits of This Creation", Carol Stream IL: Hope Publishing Co. (1970)

Dag Hammarskold, *Markings*, trans. Leif Sjoberg and W. H. Auden, New York: Alfred A. Knopf (1966) page 205.

Thich Nhat Hanh, *Thich Nhat Hanh: Essential Writings*, Robert Ellsberg (Editor), Maryknoll NY: Orbis Books (2001)

Vaclav Havel, *Letters to Olga: June 1979-September 1982*, New York: Henry Holt & Co (1989)

George Herbert (1593-1632): *The Complete English Poems*, New York: Penguin (1991)

Vicente Huidobro, *The Selected Poetry of Vicente Huidobro*, New York: New Directions Publishing Corporation (1982)

Jean Ingelow, "Sorrows Humanize Our Race" in *The Complete Poems Of Jean Ingelow (1863)* White Fish MT: Kessinger Publishing (2007); Originally published as Poems of Jean Ingelow, Boston: Roberts Brothers (1875)

Sam M. Intrator (Editor), *Living the Questions: Essays Inspired by the Work and Life of Parker J. Palmer*, San Francisco: Jossey-Bass (2005)

Sam M. Intrator and Megan Scribner (Editors), *Teaching With Fire – Poetry that Sustains the Courage to Teach*, San Francisco: Jossey-Bass (2003)

Sam M. Intrator and Megan Scribner (Editors), *Leading from Within – Poetry that Sustains the Courage to Lead*, San Francisco: Jossey-Bass (2007).

Mary Jean Irion "Normal day, let me be aware of the treasure you are" quoted in *The Quiet Voice of Soul: How to Find Meaning in Ordinary Life* (by Tian Dayton), Selinsgrove, PA: Susquehanna University Press (1995)

Sandra Joseph, *A Voice for the Child: The Inspirational Words of Janusz Korczak*, London: Thorson's Publishing (1995)

Kathy Keay (editor), *Laughter, Silence and Shouting – An Anthology of Women's Prayers*, New York: HarperCollins Publishers (1994)

Kathy Keay, "Turn Over Gently", in *Laughter, Silence and Shouting – An Anthology of Women's Prayers* (Kathy Keay, editor), New York: HarperCollins Publishers (1994) , page 43

Janusz Korczak *Ghetto Diary*, New Haven & London: Yale University Press (2003) (first published by the Holocaust Library, 1978)

Janusz Korczak "In Return," in *A Voice for the Child: The Inspirational Words of Janusz Korczak*, (Sandra Joseph), London: Thorson's Publishing (1995) page 47

Irwin Kula, *Yearnings: Embracing the Sacred Messiness of Life*, New York: Hyperion (2006)

Anne Lamott, *Traveling Mercies: Some Thoughts on Faith*, New York: Anchor Books (2000)

Patrick Lencioni, *The Five Dysfunctions of a Team: A Leadership Fable*. Hoboken, NJ: John Wiley & Sons. (2002)

Winifred M. Letts, "Prayer for a Little Child," *Songs from Leinster*, London : J. Murray (1913), page 107

Denise Levertov, "The Avowal," *The Stream and the Sapphire: Selected Poems on Religious Themes*, New York: New Directions (1997), page 6

Anne Morrow Lindbergh, *Gift from the Sea*, New York : Pantheon (1955)

Henry W. Longfellow, "As Torrents in Summer," from "The Saga of King Olav," *Tales of a Wayside Inn* White Fish MT: Kessinger Publishing (2004); Originally published 1863; New York: Houghton Mifflin Company (1913)

Clarence McConkey, "Fickle Gods of Iwo Jima," unpublished manuscript.

Tim McGraw, *Live Like You Were Dying*, Curb Records (2004)

Vassar Miller, "Morning Person," in *Struggling to Swim on Concrete*, New Orleans Poetry Journal Press (1984)

Vassar Miller, (Editor), *Despite This Flesh*, University of Texas Press (1985)

Vassar Miller, *If I had Wheels or Love*, Southern Methodist University Press (1991)

Czeslaw Milosz, "Gift," *New and Collected Poems: 1931-2001*, New York: Ecco (1988, 2001) page 277

Christopher Monger, *The Englishman Who Went Up a Hill but Came Down a Mountain*, New York: Miramax Books (1995)

Jeff Moss, "The Other Side of the Door," *The Other Side of the Door*, New York: Bantam (1991)

John Neihardt, *Black Elk Speaks*, Lincoln NE: University of Nebraska Press (1932, 1979)

Pablo Neruda, "If each day falls," *The Sea and the Bells* (William O'Daly, Translator), Port Townsend WA: Copper Canyon Press (1973, 1988): page 95

Carrie Newcomer, *The Gathering of Spirits*, Philo Music (2002)

Reinhold Niebuhr, "The Serenity Prayer," *The Essential Reinhold Niebuhr: Selected Essays and Addresses* (Robert McAfee Brown, Editor), New Have and London: Yale University Press (1986) page 251

Reinhold Niebuhr, *Moral Man and Immoral Society: A Study of Ethics and Politics*, New York: Charles Scribner's Sons (1932, 1960)

Henri J. M. Nouwen, *Bread for the Journey: A Daybook of Wisdom and Faith*, New York: HarperCollins (1997)

Marianne Novak, in *Teaching with Fire – Poetry that Sustains the Courage to Teach* (Sam M. Intrator and Megan Scribner, Editors), San Francisco: Jossey-Bass (2003), page 28

Mary Oliver, "The Summer Day", and "When Death Comes" in *New and Selected Poems*, Boston: Beacon (1992)

Mary Oliver, "The Journey," in *Dream Work*, New York: Grove/Atlantic, Inc. (1986), page 38

John O'Donohue, *Beauty: The Invisible Embrace*, New York: HarperCollins (2004)

Parker Palmer. "Heart at work: professionals who care", *Christian Century*, 124:20 (Oct. 2, 2007) pages 28-32.

Parker Palmer, *A Hidden Wholeness: The Journey Toward an Undivided Life*, San Francisco: Jossey-Bass Inc. (2004)

Parker J. Palmer, *Let Your Life Speak: Listening for the Voice of Vocation*, San Francisco: Jossey-Bass Inc. (1999)

Parker J. Palmer, *The Courage to Teach: Exploring the Inner Landscape of a Teacher's Life*, San Francisco: Jossey-Bass Inc. (1998)

Parker J. Palmer, Podcasts from the Center for Courage & Renewal, (http://www.couragerenewal.org/podcast)

Parker J. Palmer with Megan Scribner, *The Courage to Teach: A Guide for Reflection and Renewal*, San Francisco: Jossey-Bass Inc. (2007)

Parker Palmer and Tom VanderArk, preface to *Teaching with Fire – Poetry that Sustains the Courage to Teach* (Sam M. Intrator and Megan Scribner, Editors), San Francisco: Jossey-Bass (2003)

Carla Piette, "Waters of God," in *Laughter, Silence and Shouting: An Anthology of Women's Prayers* (Kathy Keay), Harper Collins (1994), page 27

Robert Pinsky and Maggie Dietz, *Poems to Read: A New Favorite Poem Project Anthology*, New York: W. W. Norton & Company (2002)

William C. Placher, Callings: *Twenty Centuries Of Christian Wisdom On Vocation*, Grand Rapids MI: Wm. B. Eerdmans Publishing Company (2005)

Rachel Naomi Remen, MD, *Kitchen Table Wisdom: Stories That Heal*, New York: Riverhead Books (1996)

Elizabeth Roberts and Elias Amidon, *Prayers for a Thousand Years*, New York: HarperCollins (1999)

Marilynne Robinson, *Gilead, A Novel*, New York: Farrar, Straus and Giroux (2004)

Archbishop Oscar Romero, "Creating the Church of Tomorrow". (Widely attributed to Archbishop Romero, this reflection was, in fact, written by Bishop Ken Untener, in conjunction with Cardinal John Dearden; see Bishop Ken Untener, *The Practical Prophet: Pastoral Writings*. Mahwah, NJ: Paulist Press (2007).)

Rumi (13th century Sufi poet): *Unseen Rain: Quatrains of Rumi* (John Moyne & Coleman, translators) Barks, Boston & London: Shambala Publications( 1986)

Rabbi Elazar ben Sammua, *Ethics of the Fathers*, (Phillip Birnbaum, Editor), NY: Hebrew Publishing Co, (1949)

Carl Sandburg, "Primer Lesson," in *The Complete Poems of Carl Sandburg*, New York: Harcourt Inc. (1970), page 306; (originally published in the collection Slabs of the Sunburnt West, New York: Harcourt, Inc., 1922)

Scott Russell Sanders, *A Private History of Awe,* New York: North Point Press (2006)

Frederica Saylor, "Doctors Debate Wisdom of Mixing Medicine and Faith," *Research News and Opportunities in Science and Theology* (November, 2003; Vol 4, No. 3), page 6

Scheer, Gene, *American Anthem*, Gene Ink Publications, www.classicalvocalrep. com (1998)

Mark R. Schwehn and Dorothy C. Bass (Editors), *Leading Lives That Matter: What We Should Do And Who We Should Be*, Grand Rapids MI: Wm. B. Eerdmans Publishing Company (2006)

Anne Sexton, "Welcome Morning," in *The Complete Poems: Anne Sexton,* New York: Houghton Mifflin Company (1981, 1999),  page 455; (originally published in the collection *The Awful Rowing Toward God*, New York: Houghton Mifflin Company, 1975)

Dave Smith, *To Be of Use: The Seven Seeds of Meaningful Work,* Novato CA: New World Library (2005)

William Stafford, "Ask Me", *The Way It Is: New & Selected Poems*, St Paul MN: Graywolf Press (1999)

Bessie Stanley, "Success," in *Heart Throbs Volume 2,* Boston, MA: Chapple Publishing Company Ltd. (1911 ); (originally published in the Lincoln Sentinel, 1905)

Robert Louis Stevenson, *A Child's Garden of Verses*, New York: Simon & Schuster (1981, 1999), (originally published by New York: Scribner, 1889); "Foreign Lands," page 15; "The Lamplighter," page 30; "Block City," page 50.

Robert Louis Stevenson, *An Inland Voyage,* White Fish MT: Kessinger Publishing Company (2004) (originally written in 1878 and published by Boston: Turner in 1905)

Eckart Tolle, *The Power of Now: A Guide to Spiritual Enlightenment*, Novato CA: New World Library (1999)

Nevin Compton Trammell, "I'm Tired, I'm Whipped," in *Cream Soda Blues: Poems for Adult Children of Life*, Brentwood TN: Cold Tree Press (2007)

Thomas H. Troeger, "Praise the Source of Faith and Learning," *Borrowed Light: Hymn Texts, Prayers, and Poems*, New York: Oxford University Press, Inc.  (1994)

Adrian Van Kaam and Susan Muto. *The Power of Appreciation: A New Approach to Personal and Relational Healing.* New York: Crossroads Publishing (1993).

Walt Whitman, "From the Debris Cluster," *Walt Whitman: Selected Poems 1855-1892*, New York: Macmillan, (1999); (originally published in Leaves of Grass, 1860)

Norman Wirzba, *Living the Sabbath: Discovering the Rhythms of Rest and Delight*, Grand Rapids MI: Brazos Press (2006)

William Wordsworth, "A primrose by a river's brim . . ." in Peter Bell, (Part 1, Stanza 12); *The Complete Poetical Works*, London: Macmillan and Co. (1888) (originally written in 1819)

# PERMISSIONS

The authors would like to express their appreciation to the following writers and their representatives who have graciously given their permission to allow selections from their writings to be included in this book.

Every effort has been made to trace the ownership of copyright items and to obtain permission for their use. The authors and publisher would appreciate notification of, and copyright details for, any instances where further acknowledgement is due, so that adjustments may be made in a future reprint.

Judy Brown, "Fire", in *Teaching with Fire – Poetry that Sustains the Courage to Teach* (Sam M. Intrator and Megan Scribner, Editors), San Francisco: Jossey-Bass (2003), page 89. Copyright © 2000, Reprinted by permission of the author.

Fred Pratt Green, "For the Fruits of This Creation", Hope Publishing Company. Copyright © 1970. Reprinted by permission of Hope Publishing Company.

Mary Jean Irion "Normal day, let me be aware of the treasure you are," quoted in *The Quiet Voice of Soul: How to Find Meaning in Ordinary Life* (by Tian Dayton), Selinsgrove, PA: Susquehanna University Press (1995). Reprinted by permission of the author.

Denise Levertov, "The Avowal," from *Oblique Prayers*. Copyright © 1984 by Denise Levertov. Reprinted by permission of New Directions Publishing Corporation.

Vassar Miller, "Morning Person," in *Struggling to Swim on Concrete,* New Orleans Poetry Journal Press (1984). Copyright © 1984. Reprinted by permission of publisher.

Czeslaw Milosz, "Gift," *New and Collected Poems: 1931-2001*, New York: Ecco. Copyright © 1988. Reprinted by permission of HarperCollins Publishing.

Pablo Neruda, "If each day falls," translated by William O'Daly from *The Sea and the Bells.* Copyright © 1973 by Pablo Neruda, Fundacion Pablo Neruda. Translation copyright © 1989 by William O'Daly. Reprinted with the permissionof Copper Canyon Press, www.coppercanyonpress.org.

Carrie Newcomer, *The Gathering of Spirits*, Philo Music (2002). Copyright © 2002. Lyrics from the compositions entitled "I'll Go Too" and "The Gathering of Spirits" reprinted by permission of the author.

LaVergne, TN USA
11 June 2010
185901LV00001B/8/P